THE
STATE-LINE
MOB

THE
STATE-LINE
MOB

A True Story of Murder and Intrigue

W. R. Morris

RUTLEDGE HILL PRESS
Nashville, Tennessee

*This book is lovingly dedicated to my wife,
Cathy "Sue" Morris.*

Published in Nashville, Tennessee, by Rutledge Hill Press,
513 Third Avenue South, Nashville, Tennessee 37210

Typography by Bailey Typography, Inc., Nashville, Tennessee

Library of Congress Cataloging-in-Publication Data

Morris, W. R., 1934-
    The state-line mob : a true story of murder and intrigue / W. R.
Morris.
        p.   cm.
    ISBN 1-55853-082-7
    1. Crime—Tennessee—McNairy County—History—20th century.
    2. Crime—Mississippi—Alcorn County—History—20th century.
    I. Title.
    HV6795.M36M67   1990
    364.1'06'09762993—dc20   90-46608
                                                               CIP

Printed in the United States of America
1 2 3 4 5 6 7 8 — 96 95 94 93 92 91 90

INTRODUCTION

During the early 1950s, a hotbed of crime straddled the border between McNairy County, Tennessee, and Alcorn County, Mississippi. Gambling, prostitution, bootlegging, and arbitrary violence flourished nonstop in the cheap state-line dives. Murders were committed regularly on the strip, which was a stopping-off point for criminals hiding from the law. Tourists constantly complained of being robbed, and weighted bodies were often found in the nearby Tennessee River.

Midway through the 1950s, a new gang of outlaws settled in the state-line joints when authorities closed the gambling casinos and whorehouses in Phenix City, Alabama.

The Hathcocks, who had risen from the backwash of poverty to the top of the criminal ladder, were the state-line overlords. Jack and Louise Hathcock operated dives in both Tennessee and Mississippi. Jack's nephew, W. O. Hathcock, Jr., and his wife, Larice, ran a dance hall near the border on Mississippi soil. The establishments thrived on harlots, illegal booze, and shakedown rackets.

Those who "raised too much hell" about being swindled were dealt with harshly. If the bilked men could not be persuaded to "forget the whole deal," they were often severely beaten or murdered.

Many complaints about the state-line corruption and strong-arm executions were lodged with the authorities at the courthouses in Selmer, Tennessee, and Corinth, Mississippi. Cases were usually thrown out of court due to scanty evidence or because key witnesses were paid off.

In the early 1960s, a young outlaw named Carl Douglas "Towhead" White hooked up with the state-line mob. Fresh out of prison, he vowed to become the Al Capone of the South.

Jack and Louise Hathcock had a booming business at the Shamrock Restaurant and Motel. The restaurant was in Mississippi, and the motel was right next door, just across the line in Tennessee. White quickly muscled in on the illegal activities. Louise decided to divorce Jack.

Towhead White and Louise Hathcock became lovers, and when her ex-husband objected to the relationship, the flamboyant young gangster drilled Jack Hathcock full of bullet holes. Towhead and Louise were the only witnesses to the slaying. She told the authorities that she had shot her ex-husband in self-defense, and the murder charges that had been lodged against her were dropped.

Buford Pusser pinned on the McNairy County sheriff's badge in 1964 and immediately locked horns with Towhead White and Louise Hathcock. Less than two years later, Pusser was forced to kill Mrs. Hathcock in a shoot-out at the Shamrock Motel. Her death ignited a violent feud between Buford Pusser and Towhead White.

On August 12, 1967, White masterminded an ambush that left Pusser sprawled at the edge of eternity and his wife, Pauline, a corpse. The sheriff survived the assassination attempt and swore that White would pay severely for every drop of blood Pauline Pusser had lost.

Minutes after midnight on April 3, 1969, Carl Douglas "Towhead" White was gunned down at a Corinth motel. Another hoodlum named Berry "Junior" Smith claimed he killed White in self-defense. Actually, the murder had been instigated and planned by Buford Pusser.

I have been collecting this information for more than twenty years. I was personally acquainted with many of the outlaws who nested in the dives along the Tennessee–Mississippi border. I crossed paths with them while I was doing research for Buford Pusser's authorized biography, *The Twelfth of August*. Pusser fought the state-line criminals during his entire six-year reign as sheriff of McNairy County, Tennessee.

During the state-line wars, Pusser created a larger-than-life image. But while walking tall, he often walked outside the law.

Members of the state-line mob were bold and colorful. They lived hard and fast. Most of them died the same way.

—W. R. Morris

ACKNOWLEDGMENTS

This is strictly a work of nonfiction, based entirely on factual material, personal interviews, and years of research. It is a true story about real people. Only the identities of some of the victims have been concealed.

The names of almost everyone who provided me with information are mentioned in the book, and for that reason, I will not identify them here.

There are certain persons whose contributions to my work are special: Cathy Meadows, my most trusted assistant; Maxene McDaniel; Ed Metzer; James Harvell; Fred Plunk; James Minton; Bill Card; Gene Swearingen; Ron Windsor; Charles F. Scott; Billy Wagoner; Charles E. Reynolds; Vicki Sweat; Grady Bingham; and Roy and Ruth Wallace.

WRM

THE
STATE-LINE
MOB

"... for all they that take the sword shall perish with the sword."

—Matthew 26:52

CHAPTER ONE

Towhead White awoke at noon. Shuffling into the kitchen, he downed a cup of black instant Folgers, then telephoned Billy Garrett's downtown shoe shop. Garrett, who excelled in peddling stolen merchandise, answered.

"Hey, Billy. What's happenin'? Thought you'd be out makin' a score someplace," White laughed.

"Already made one. Got a load of hot shoes to stock. All of 'em are first-class footwear."

Both White and Garrett were members of the state-line mob who specialized in fleecing honky-tonkers along the Tennessee-Mississippi border. White was a seasoned criminal with major league credentials. Garrett was still working his way up from the minors.

"Well, put Pearl on the line and get your ass back to work."

"I believe yore hung up on that nigger gal, Tow. She is good-lookin'. Ain't a movie star in Hollywood that looks any better."

"Quit runnin' your mouth, Garrett, and let me talk to Pearl," snapped White. He resented any teasing about his relationship with the young mulatto woman.

"Damn! You don't have to bite my head off! Here she is!"

The gangster quickly arranged to pick Pearl up from work, then cradled the phone.

White had been dating the attractive, olive-skinned black girl for several weeks. He thought he might be in love with her, but he had a serious problem. Sheriff Buford Pusser was also having an affair with Pearl.

White intended to have a heart-to-heart talk with his

girlfriend about the McNairy County sheriff. The more he thought about Pusser and himself sharing the same forbidden fruit, the angrier Towhead became. He hated Buford Pusser more than any other person he knew.

When the flamboyant outlaw picked up his date from work, his temperature had reached the mercury-shattering mark. His jealousy was boiling, and he wasted no time spewing it out. "Pearl, why in the hell do you keep fuckin' with Buford Pusser? You don't need him. Hell, you don't even have to work. I'll take care of you!

"Besides, I really love you, Pearl. Pusser don't give a damn about you. He's gonna play with you till he decides to get a new toy. Then he's gonna toss you aside like a used rubber."

The young woman watched a flock of crows flutter from a splattered opossum carcass on the road as White's Cadillac approached it. She remained silent. Pearl did not want to discuss her relationship with Buford Pusser. Actually, she enjoyed his company and thought of him as a kind, gentle man.

"You know I'm tellin' you the truth about Pusser. He's just using you, little darlin'."

Pearl twisted around on the car seat and faced White. "Towhead, I came with you tonight to have a good time, not to be cross-examined about Buford Pusser."

"I know why you're spreadin' them pretty little legs for Pusser. You think he'll keep the heat off of your uncle's beer joint," White smirked.

Pearl's uncle operated a black dive near the Tennessee-Mississippi border. She had met the sheriff there.

"That's a lie!" she shot back. "I like Buford Pusser. Just because you hate his guts is no sign I have to."

"Come on, level with me. What's your big attraction to Pusser?"

"Towhead! I've already told you. I'm not gonna discuss him tonight. Now, if you're gonna keep insistin' on it, you can just take me on home!"

White knew he had pushed Pearl to the edge of irritability, and he did not want to alienate himself from her completely. He dropped the Pusser subject.

Close associates of Towhead White had often chided him

for dating a black woman after claiming he despised members of her race. The hoodlum justified his actions by saying the woman was more Caucasian than black.

Sunup was approaching when White delivered Pearl to her front door. In spite of a rocky start, the couple had spent another "honeymoon night" together. More fuel had been poured onto the coals of hatred that smoldered between the outlaw and the sheriff.

CHAPTER TWO

•

The state line rambled across U.S. Highway 45. It wandered through tall pine thickets and split rich farmlands, forcing the owners to pay taxes in both McNairy County, Tennessee, and Alcorn County, Mississippi.

The area was virtually flat with a few small hills peeping from the landscape. The countryside was dotted with modest, well-kept houses and large barns. Occasionally, a steepled church rose from the horizon.

Most people in that rural region earned a living on a farm tractor or by raising hogs and cattle. Some cut the native oak, poplar, and pine timber or labored at the sawmills. A few worked in small factories. The majority were God-fearing folk.

The drone of the tractors, the smell of freshly turned earth, and the keen scent of fallen pine needles all betrayed the evil environment of the state line. In the honky-tonks near the border, criminal wrongdoing flourished around the clock. The shoddy dives were the topic of a hell-and-brimstone sermon in at least one area church every Sunday.

With the birth of the 1950s, corruption at the state line swelled, a fact blamed partly on the migration of several undesirable characters from Phenix City, Alabama. Officials of the Yellowhammer State, using National Guard muscle, had closed the gambling halls and whorehouses that once thrived on the army paychecks from nearby Fort Benning, Georgia. Many of the shakedown artists who were chased from Phenix City had settled in the roadhouses at the crime-infested Mississippi–Tennessee border. It was a rowdy strip of live wires, and its demise was nowhere in sight.

14

Actually, Alcorn County citizens had helped to build the "hell holes" themselves by voting the county bone dry in the 1940s. In fact, the entire state of Mississippi was legally dry at that time. Beer and whiskey sales were illegal in McNairy County as well, although intoxicating beverages could be lawfully purchased in some other parts of Tennessee.

Bootleggers, inspired by the whiskey prohibitions, staked their solid claims in liquid gold mines. Liquor opponents soon learned that people were going to drink intoxicants whether it was lawful or not, and while the state and county governments lost a fortune in tax dollars, the unlicensed booze peddlers mopped up.

The Hathcock gang members were the state-line overlords. They had built a far-flung outlaw enterprise with bootlegged whiskey as the centerpiece. The Hathcocks were old pros in the racketeering game, and the only schemes they had not pulled were those that had not yet been discovered.

Jack and Louise Hathcock owned the Forty-Five Grill, a large restaurant and dance hall just inside the Mississippi line.

Across U.S. Highway 45, also on Mississippi soil, sat the Plantation Club, owned by W. O. Hathcock, Jr. (Jack's nephew), and his wife, Larice.

The Hathcocks also operated a couple of joints across the Tennessee border. The dives had been officially closed by the authorities, but that did not stop the state-line mob from gambling and bootlegging there.

Seldom did a McNairy County Court session pass without the Hathcocks or some of their hooligans appearing on the docket for transporting whiskey, storing beer for resale, or operating a gambling house. The thugs were also frequently arrested in Alcorn County for robbery, bootlegging, gambling, and criminal assaults. The cases were usually thrown out of court for inadequate evidence or because key witnesses failed to show. When cases actually were tried, the fines assessed were modest.

Law enforcement officials at the courthouses in Selmer, Tennessee, and Corinth, Mississippi, considered the Hathcocks to be "one big pain in the ass." It was easier to squeeze toothpaste back into the tube than it was to gather enough hard evidence to convict the Hathcocks. They were wizards at devising ironclad alibis.

When Jack and Louise opened the doors of the Forty-Five Grill in 1950, they lured tourists to their business with road signs advertising "country ham, red-eye gravy, and homemade biscuits." After the unsuspecting travelers enjoyed a home-cooked southern meal, the Hathcocks and their thugs would coax them into playing three-card monte or taking a trip to a rigged dice table.

The card game involved picking the only red-faced pasteboard from a spread of three placed face down by the dealer after a quick shuffle on a tabletop. The "house man" always knew exactly where the red card was. The old "the hand is quicker than the eye" trick, coupled with their crooked dice games, netted the Hathcocks more than $3,500 each week.

Gambling was not the only sin that filled the Hathcock coffers. Young whores enticed male customers with their flirty smiles and short, skintight dresses. A fast romp in the sack usually cost twenty dollars, and those who balked at spending the extra price for comfort in a nearby tourist cabin wallowed with the Jezebels in the rear seats of cars. A "quickie," with no assurance of privacy, was also available in a back room of the honky-tonk.

When the harvest was wrapped up, many area farmers journeyed to the state line, where they bedded harlots, gambled, and consumed large amounts of bootlegged whiskey. Several of them "lost their crops" each year at the Mississippi–Tennessee border.

The Forty-Five Grill was a long, one-story frame building with white asbestos shingle siding. The restaurant was situated in the middle of the establishment. On the north end sat a dance hall/game room combination. The main ballroom occupied the southern portion of the spacious structure. Each area had a separate entrance from the outside. Green-and-white striped awnings decorated the front windows and doors.

A long span of metal affixed to the roof, compliments of Coca-Cola, advertised: "Steak. Chicken. Sandwiches."

From the outside, the Forty-Five Grill looked like an ordinary restaurant and dance hall. Inside it was a den of crooked card games, prostitution, and rigged dice tables. Violence often erupted, leaving "customers" badly beaten and, on some occasions, dead.

Three narrow, upright neon signs proclaimed: "45 Grill," "Cafe," and "Dine—Dance."

Directly across the highway, a V-shaped billboard boasted: "Welcome. Country Ham. Eggs. Red-Eye Gravy and Hot Biscuits. Enjoy a Southern Style Breakfast. Only 49¢." Similar placards had been erected alongside major highways throughout the area. Many times, the Hathcocks barely broke even on the meals, but once the tourists had swallowed the bait, the sky was the limit.

Jack Hathcock arrived at the Forty-Five Grill before 8:00 A.M., two hours earlier than his usual check-in time. A load of Missouri-taxed whiskey would soon be arriving, and he needed to inventory it.

Born Clyde Raymond Hathcock on July 26, 1920, in Michie, Tennessee, he was known to everyone, for some unexplained reason, as "Jack." Even his legal documents bore the name Jack Hathcock.

He was tall and slender with a full head of dark brown hair, and he was almost illiterate, but likable. From birth, his speech had been flawed by an impediment that had gradually improved with age.

A neat dresser, he usually wore expensive slacks and sport shirts. On his left hand, he flashed a large, almost gaudy, diamond ring. He chain-smoked Rio-Tan cigars.

Jack Hathcock was lily-livered to the core. He hired other hoodlums to do his dirty work, and when trouble exploded in the Forty-Five Grill, he let Louise tame the rowdy customers.

Slightly older than her husband, Louise was medium built, had a large bust, and wore her dark brown hair short. She was as mean as a two-headed rattlesnake. Everyone, especially Jack, knew that she ruled the roost at the Forty-Five Grill.

Louise seldom wore dresses. Her usual attire consisted of black uniform-style slacks and tops. She was rarely without her white two-pocket apron that contained an order pad, a retractable ink pen, and a ball peen hammer.

When Jack had counted and stashed the bootlegged whiskey, he seated himself at a corner table with Berry "Junior" Smith and Oliver Lee "Nimbo" Price.

The nineteen-year-old Smith worked at the Forty-Five Grill. A native of Boyle, Mississippi, he had migrated from the Delta to the Corinth area with another thug named Carl Douglas "Towhead" White. When White was not on the road stealing, he also worked at the grill.

Price, who was only sixteen, had been born in Corinth. A high school dropout, he spent his time running errands and doing odd jobs for the Hathcocks.

Louise Hathcock sauntered in.

"Hey. You guys look like a hard workin' crew. Y'all need to slow down. I wouldn't want any of you to keel over with a heart attack," she laughed as she made her way to the kitchen. She was carrying a grocery sack.

"What's in the bag?" Jack asked.

"Lettuce, tomatoes, and green peppers. We are flat out of anything to fix salads with."

Minutes before noon, a lanky, middle-aged timber buyer named Claude Sanders entered the restaurant and seated himself near the door. He lived in Little Rock, Arkansas, and this was his first visit to the Forty-Five Grill.

Louise slid from a stool behind a long, Formica-covered counter. She scooped some ice from a bin into a glass, added water, and picked up a menu.

"How are you today, sir?" she purred, placing the ice water and the menu on a red-and-white checkered table-cloth.

"Fine. I'll try one of your T-bone steaks, rare, with French fries," he said without looking at the menu. The timber man figured that anyone who advertised steaks on an outdoor sign should have any kind a person wanted.

"Oh . . . do you sell beer?" he asked.

"You're not one of them A.B.C. [Alcoholic Beverage Control] boys, are you?" Louise smiled.

"No, ma'am. I buy trees for a company out of Arkansas."

"What kind you want?"

"Bring me a Miller."

After Sanders ate his steak and washed it down with two beers, he paid his bill. Before he could leave, Junior Smith summoned him to his table.

"You want to make some easy money?" Smith asked.

Sanders hesitated. "I'm always interested in makin' easy money. What's the catch?"

"There ain't no catch. I'll bet you can't open this knife ever' time you try," said Smith, handing the shiv to Sanders so he could inspect it.

The timber buyer easily opened and closed the blade several times.

"See. It's just an ordinary knife," Smith assured him.

"Seems too easy to open. What's the trick?"

"There ain't no trick, man. That knife won't open every time. It hangs up. I'm bettin' on the odds."

Sanders ordered another beer.

"I'll bet you ten dollars you can't open that damned knife," Smith challenged.

Sanders, still holding the knife, laid a ten-spot on the table. With no effort, he pulled open the blade.

"Let's bet another ten dollars," Smith frowned.

"Okay. My money is down." Sanders retrieved his original ten but left his winnings on the table.

Smith allowed the timber man to win sixty dollars. Then he persuaded Sanders to let him up the ante. "Let's bet a hundred dollars this go 'round. I've been like a one-legged man at an ass kickin' so far. It's about time your luck changed," Smith predicted.

"I feel lucky as a shithouse rat. You're on," laughed Sanders. He tossed two twenty-dollar bills into the sixty dollar pot.

Smith, who had picked up the knife after the last bet, pressed a hidden lock on the handle. He gave it back to Sanders.

The tree buyer attempted several times to yank open the blade.

"You don't get to pull on it all night. You lose," Smith smiled as he scooped up the cash from the table. "I knew your luck would run out sooner or later. Let's bet another hundred."

Sanders, believing that the blade had simply stuck by some quirk of fate, called the bet. After dropping three hundred dollars, some of it company funds, Sanders flew off the handle. "This damned deal must be rigged."

Louise Hathcock hurried toward the table.

"Somethin's wrong. You did somethin' to that knife blade. A tow truck couldn't open that damned blade now. There's a lock on it somewhere. You stole my money!" Sanders protested.

"Listen, you sonofabitch! You got a lotta nerve comin' in here and callin' us thieves," Louise yelled.

Jack, armed with a .357-magnum, moved in behind his wife.

"I'm just callin' a spade a spade," Sanders insisted.

Louise removed the ball peen hammer from her apron. "I'm gonna teach you some manners, boy. I don't appreciate you comin' in here and accusin' us of stealin'," she hissed as she smashed the man's skull repeatedly with the hammer.

Sanders locked his arms around his head and face in an attempt to protect himself from the blows. Then Jack slammed the magnum down on the top of his head. Sanders slumped unconscious to the floor in a pool of blood.

Jack rifled the man's pockets of another six hundred dollars, then removed his diamond-studded wristwatch. Sanders was wearing no other jewelry. With Sanders' pockets turned inside out, Jack, Junior, and Nimbo dragged him through the back door into an empty dirt lot behind the restaurant.

When the timber man regained consciousness, he struggled to his feet, found his Dodge pickup, and sped away. He had no intention of reporting the crime to the sheriff. That would require facing the Hathcocks in court. Sanders was terrified. He was convinced that if he did prosecute, the state-line mob would murder him.

A similar incident occurred at the Forty-Five Grill on Wednesday, May 6, 1953. Once again, Junior Smith and Nimbo Price were there.

Morgan Wallins, a Memphis insurance salesman, stopped by the grill for a cheeseburger and French fries. When he finished eating, he paid for the meal with money from his wallet, then cashed a $105 company check.

Before Wallins could leave, Jack and Louise Hathcock beat and robbed him. They took his money and a diamond Masonic ring valued at one hundred dollars.

The salesman was not as easily frightened as the timber buyer had been. He drove straight to Sheriff Bobby Phillips's office in Corinth.

When the sheriff went to the Forty-Five Grill to arrest the Hathcocks, they were out of pocket. Word quickly reached the outlaws that robbery warrants had been issued for them, and they voluntarily surrendered to the authorities. Peace Justice Joe Gray released them on bonds of $10,000 each.

On July 13, 1953, the Alcorn County grand jury indicted the Hathcocks for robbery. Louise immediately contacted Wallins and offered to pay him $500 for his $105 loss and to return his Masonic ring. The salesman accepted her bribe, and the case was scratched from the court docket.

Days later, a thirty-five-year-old Georgia man, the victim of another robbery, was found lying alongside Highway 45 on the Mississippi side of the border. Brutally beaten, he refused to identify his assailants.

Complaints about the Forty-Five Grill and other state-line joints did not fall on deaf ears at the Alcorn County Courthouse in Corinth. County Attorney James Price and other officials frequently sorted through options that might effectively purify the strip of crime.

Sheriff Bobby Phillips decided to have a conference with Jack Hathcock. Phillips—big, bald, and heavyset—was a man of few words. He never took the long way around getting to the bottom line on any subject. "Hathcock, me and everybody else at the courthouse are fed up with your shit. All of these robberies, assaults, and shakedown rackets had better come to a screeching halt," announced Phillips. "If they don't, I'm going to padlock this damned joint and throw your ass in jail!"

CHAPTER THREE

Trying to threaten Jack Hathcock into joining the ranks of law-abiding citizens was like trying to drown a duck by flinging it into a river.

Hathcock was a state-line veteran. He had worked at the crime strip ever since he was barely sixteen years old. L. A. "Kay" Timlake, a prosperous Corinth jukebox operator, had placed Jack on the payroll at his State-Line Club in 1936. Timlake hired Hathcock fresh from the Tennessee Reformatory in Nashville, where he had been locked up when he was fifteen for pilfering houses in McNairy County.

The State-Line Club, a crude, off-white block building, straddled the border. Part of it was in Tennessee; the other portion, in Mississippi.

Although Jack was not even old enough to shave regularly, he learned the ropes quickly. He hoodwinked the customers, tapped the cash register, and sidestepped personal arguments that might provoke fistfights. While Jack was uneducated and a born coward, he was far from being the "village idiot." He was already planning someday to own the club in which he worked.

Timlake was impressed with Jack Hathcock's scrappy attitude and ambition. Even though the young bandit was dipping into the money drawer, the joint was raking in more greenbacks than it ever had. Business had increased since the shifty, well-liked juvenile delinquent began working there.

Midway through 1937 Jack met Louise Anderson at the club, and she immediately captured his undivided attention. He thought she was the most attractive girl he had ever

23

laid eyes on, and he assured himself that he was going to marry "that ole gal come hell or high water." Her formfitting gray slacks, so tight they revealed the outline of her underwear, and her bulging red blouse hoisted his determination to win Louise's affections.

Hathcock quickly persuaded Kay Timlake to put his new-found heartthrob on the payroll. Louise had come from West Point, Mississippi, to the state line seeking financial security. Although the Depression was petering out, the South was still feeling its pinch in 1937. Good jobs were few and far between.

Many men who had steady employment blew their paychecks at the state-line joints. Their wives and children often went without proper clothing and food.

After Louise assumed her waitress job, Jack worked hard to impress her. His promises to "own the club someday" always sparked her interest in him. Occasionally, he flashed the large roll of cash he kept in his right front pants pocket—more money than Louise had seen in her entire life.

In less than three months, Jack asked Louise to exchange wedding vows with him. She reluctantly accepted his proposal.

Louise Anderson did not want to spend the rest of her life with Jack Hathcock. But neither did she want to spend the rest of her life wondering where her next meal was coming from.

In her early teens Louise had decided that money, not love, would lure her to the altar. She had been searching for a man of means, and she had found a few. But all they ever gave her was empty promises and one-night stands in strange motel beds.

Louise was born on March 19, 1919, in West Point. Her parents, Shelton and Bessie Anderson, had moved to the small Mississippi town from Richmond, Kentucky, before Louise's birth. She was next to the youngest of five children—three boys and two girls. During the Depression years, Shelton had struggled to support his family by raising cattle on a small farm in Clay County near West Point. Times had been tough for the Andersons, and they were not much better when Louise left home.

Louise Hathcock was as mean as a two-headed rattlesnake, and she had a split personality as well. She would lend a helping hand to the needy one day, then kill a person in cold blood the next.

On October 3, 1937, in Corinth, Mississippi, Laura Louise Anderson became Mrs. Jack Hathcock. Both lied about their ages on the marriage license application. Louise, who was eighteen, claimed she was a year older, and Jack, who was only seventeen, swore that he was twenty-one.

The couple moved into a small rental house owned by Kay Timlake. Louise was conservative with money, but Jack was a relentless penny pincher. People often joked that "old Abe" screamed each time Jack got his hands on him.

Poverty had scarred and molded Jack Hathcock at an early age. His parents, Will and Janie Hathcock, had toiled in the cotton fields to rear Jack and his five sisters and four brothers. Spare change around the Hathcock homestead was as scarce as silver dollars in a wino's pocket.

The Hathcock farm, less than forty acres, was near Michie, a tiny settlement in southeastern McNairy County, Tennessee.

Jack picked up spending money by bootlegging moonshine whiskey. He peddled the booze from saddlebags on the white horse he rode to the Michie Elementary School, but he rarely attended classes. Usually, he sold the liquor to his young "clients" on the school yard, then left.

The Hathcocks were not a closely knit family. Will, who suffered from jake leg, a paralysis triggered by drinking large amounts of rotgut whiskey, was hot tempered. He often quarreled and fought with other members of his household, and it seemed especially difficult for him to cultivate a smooth relationship with his twin sons, Isdo and Edow. He always found himself crossways with one or the other or both.

On the night of May 12, 1934, a feud erupted between Isdo and his father when Will cursed Janie Hathcock and threatened to "beat the hell out of" her. Isdo immediately defended his mother, who left during the argument and sought refuge in Corinth at the home of her eldest son, Odell. Before Isdo left for the same destination, he snatched a pistol from its hiding place under Will's pillow and smashed his father in the head with it.

Will Hathcock doctored his wounds with rubbing alcohol, bandaged his head with a piece of a torn bed sheet, and went to his daughter's home in Corinth. Before he left for Mississippi, he borrowed a .32-caliber handgun from his neighbor Casey Farris.

The following morning, Will Hathcock parked his black Model-A Ford in front of Odell's store in Corinth. He knew that both his wife and Isdo had spent the night at Odell's house.

Odell Hathcock sold groceries, beer, and whiskey. At that time, the sale of alcoholic beverages in Corinth was legal. Isdo worked for his brother at the store. Will called Isdo outside.

As the young man approached his father's car, Will flung open the door and shot his twenty-five-year-old son in the chest with the .32-caliber pistol. Isdo stumbled backward, but before he fell, another shot shattered the Sunday morning silence. Seconds later, Will Hathcock, at age fifty-five, lay dead beneath the opened door of his Model-A. Isdo Hathcock died the next day.

Many people believed that Odell killed his father to

avenge his brother's slaying. Authorities concluded that the two relatives died in an exchange of gunfire.

When Casey Farris loaned the weapon to Will Hathcock, he had no idea that his friend would use it to murder one of his twin sons and that Will himself would end up in the nearby Carter Cemetery.

Violence continued to plague the Hathcocks. It seemed to run in their family. Jack's sister Pearl, for instance, later stabbed her boyfriend to death with an ice pick. She escaped conviction.

In the early 1940s Kay Timlake agreed to sell the State-Line Club to Jack Hathcock. Timlake, who had grown extremely fond of the young hooligan, practically gave him the club. The property included the building and ten acres of land divided by the Mississippi–Tennessee state line.

Rumors circulated that Jack had stolen the real estate from Timlake when the wealthy landowner plunged into hot water with the Internal Revenue Service. Before the I.R.S. could drop the net on Timlake, he transferred ownership of his properties into the names of trusted friends and relatives. The State-Line Club was deeded to Hathcock. Then, according to hearsay, Hathcock kept the property when Timlake settled his I.R.S. account.

Even if Jack Hathcock had been tempted to swindle Timlake, he would have never risked the dangerous repercussions. Wicked as Satan himself, Kay Timlake had already put several persons in Boot Hill, and Hathcock knew that he would be next if he double-crossed the old tycoon.

Meanwhile, bootlegging, whore-hopping, gambling, and the shakedown rackets continued to thrive at the sin-laden establishment twenty-four hours a day.

Before McNairy County dried up, other members of the state-line mob had operated a cluster of joints in Tennessee near the border, most of them financed by Jack Hathcock.

Dewitt Curtis and Howard Carroll ran a dive called the Dusty Star. Activities at the Golden Rule were directed by Melton Deberry. W. O. Hathcock, Jr., and Everett "Pee Wee" Walker managed the Hill Top Inn.

Toward the end of 1948 McNairy County Sheriff Hugh

Kirkpatrick and deputies John Donahoe and R. B. "Bruce" Leonard started cracking the whip at the state line.

With the assistance of Attorney General George Watkins, the sheriff obtained a court order from Circuit Court Judge Mark A. Walker to close the dives near the Tennessee border. On November 26, 1948, McNairy County authorities padlocked all the state-line joints, including Jack Hathcock's place.

In spite of the court order, Jack and Louise continued to operate. On January 10, 1949, McNairy County law enforcement officers raided the Hathcocks and seized thirteen cases of beer.

Jack's bold decision to defy the authorities had angered the sheriff and the attorney general. While the officials pondered what action to take, the Hathcocks abandoned the State-Line Club. The authorities thought they had moved from the area. The racketeers, however, were merely out of town attending to some personal business.

In West Point, the wife of Louise Hathcock's youngest brother had died giving birth. Louise, who was infertile, wanted to adopt the baby girl, who had been named Jeanette Susan. After some discussion with Louise's brother, William Anderson, an agreement was sealed. The infant later became the legally adopted daughter of the Hathcocks.

McNairy County law enforcement officers had been watching the State-Line Club like hungry foxes eyeing a chicken house. When the Hathcocks returned, they heard from other state-line sources that the McNairy County law had been "practically living" at the padlocked club.

Jack Hathcock, realizing that the party was over at his joint on the Tennessee–Mississippi border, leveled it with dynamite. Before the dust had settled from the explosion, he was making plans to build a brand-new joint there.

Because Hathcock knew that he had to deceive the McNairy County authorities into believing he had washed his hands clean of the places along the border, he "sold" the property where his old club had sat to his brother-in-law William Anderson for one hundred dollars. The transaction was a sham from the outset. The real estate never belonged to Anderson except on paper at the courthouses in Selmer and Corinth, and no money ever exchanged hands. The private arrangement was for Anderson to deed back the property whenever Hathcock asked him to do so.

In the meantime, McNairy County suspended the legal sale of beer. Liquor sales had never been lawful there.

Within months Jack Hathcock had constructed a large restaurant and dance hall and called it the Forty-Five Grill. It was built on state-line property but situated entirely in Alcorn County.

CHAPTER FOUR

Kinnie Wagner heard the distinct noise in the distance. No other tractor, he thought, had its own distinctive sound like an old John Deere. Its two-cylinder engine, always coughing loudly, never ran smoothly.

It was nearing the end of fall in 1953, and farmers were hurrying to disc under their cornstalks before winter arrived with its short days and long nights.

Born in Scott County, Virginia, Wagner was familiar with rural life. And until four years earlier, he had driven tractors and performed other chores in the state-owned cotton fields at Parchman, Mississippi.

Although Wagner roamed the countryside, he was not a free man. He still owed the state of Mississippi a life sentence for five murder convictions.

The news media had made his name a household word. Journalists and others claimed he was the "fastest gun" in the South. Not since the days of Jesse James had one man attracted so much attention. Fortunately for Kinnie Wagner, his name was more widely known than his face.

The sounds of the John Deere grew louder as Wagner lumbered toward the Tennessee–Mississippi state line.

Wagner, who was hiding out at a friend's house less than two miles away, had walked to the state border. It was almost dusky dark, and he planned to drink a few beers and enjoy some female companionship. He kept his distance from the women with whom he was well acquainted. It was unfair, he believed, to foster an intimate relationship with a lady when his entire future waited for him behind jail bars.

Although Wagner had never before darkened the doors of

the Forty-Five Grill, he recognized it from traveling with friends in automobiles on U.S. Highway 45. He knew from various reports, some of them firsthand, that the dive had an evil reputation.

Outside the rear entrance to the dance hall, he patted the .38-caliber pistol he kept holstered on a prison-made leather belt. The weapon was well hidden under a long-tailed Western coat. His almost new, but scuffed, boots were a gift from a former Parchman inmate with whom he had once pulled time. His brown wide-brimmed hat needed reblocking.

Wagner was tall, well over six feet. Except for his graying temples, he looked much younger than his fifty years of age.

Inside the crowded ballroom, a skinny waitress led him to a corner table, where he ordered a Budweiser. In his right bottom coat pocket, he had seventy-two dollars, money he had earned from doing odd jobs.

Before Wagner could finish his first beer, one of Jack Hathcock's employees, a young blonde girl, approached him. "Howdy, good lookin'. You want to dance?" she smiled.

Wagner stood.

"Sure. Maybe I won't step all over your toes," he laughed.

After the slow, belly-hugging dance, Wagner returned to his table while the girl melted into the crowd.

When the fugitive went to order another beer, he discovered that his money was gone. He knew immediately that the teenage girl, who had been all over him on the dance floor, had lifted it. Apparently, she had seen where he kept his cash when he paid for his beer. Or the waitress had tipped her off.

Wagner quickly located the skinny waitress and asked to see the owner. She pointed to Jack Hathcock, who was sitting at the bar with Pee Wee Walker and two other thugs.

The prison escapee strolled to within reach of Hathcock. "Excuse me. You the owner?" Wagner asked in a polite voice.

"That's me."

"I wanted to tell you that one of your girls swiped my money while we were dancin' out there."

Anger flushed Hathcock's face. "I don't like that kinda

talk. How you know it was one of my girls who ripped you off?"

Wagner remained calm. "She told me she worked for you. Said her name was Judy."

"She don't work for me. I don't like your attitude. Comin' in here accusin' me of havin' hired hands who are thieves."

"The girl said she worked for you. She stole my money. I want it back."

Hathcock glanced at Walker and the two hoodlums beside him. "Listen, and listen real good. You'd better get your ass outta here while you're still in one piece. We don't put up with nobody comin' in here callin' us crooks. Get outta here right now!" demanded Hathcock.

"You know who I am?"

"No. I don't give a fuck who you are. Now get your ass out before you get hurt real bad."

"I'm Kinnie Wagner."

Jack Hathcock turned white. He quickly recognized the name of the notorious gunslinger, and he wanted no quarrel with him.

Wagner was not nearly as fast on the draw as Hathcock was at switching from vinegar to honey. "Which one of them girls took your money? Point her out to me. I'll nail her ass right now!" promised Hathcock.

"I haven't seen her since we danced. She seems to have disappeared into thin air."

"How much did you lose?"

"Had seventy-two dollars when I came in. Bought a beer. That left me seventy-one dollars."

Hathcock knew that "his ole gal" would not return to the dance hall until her victim departed. He reached into his right front pants pocket and slipped out a roll of cash. "Here's seventy-five dollars. Keep the change for your trouble. Sorry you got fleeced. It's hard to watch all these greedy little whores hangin' around here. When I catch 'em robbin' customers, I run their asses off."

"I appreciate you givin' my money back," Wagner said as he headed toward the door. He wanted to leave the joint before he was forced to shoot one of the "crooked bastards." He told himself that there were more outlaws in the

Forty-Five Grill than there were in the state penitentiary at Parchman.

Kinnie Wagner was not trigger-happy. Nor was he a bully who used his expert marksmanship to boost his ego. His Jesse James reputation concealed his true character as a southern gentleman.

Wagner had escaped from Parchman on March 15, 1948, and wandered through five different states before returning to Mississippi. He had survived the five-year manhunt by working at odd jobs, camping in the woods, and receiving help from his friends.

One of Wagner's close associates was Clovis Eaton. Clovis and his brother Ruey were prominent outlaws in northern Mississippi. They were from the Dry Creek Hills area near Booneville.

The Eatons had met Wagner in Parchman while they, too, were doing time for murder. Clovis and Kinnie became as close as two peas in a pod.

Later, when Clovis had been released from custody and Kinnie was on the run, the authorities arrested Eaton and charged him with harboring Wagner. He beat the rap.

Like Wagner, Ruey Eaton had fled the Parchman cotton fields. He was arrested while on the lam and later convicted of federal car theft charges. He was sent to Alcatraz, where he shared a cell with former Mafia kingpin Al Capone.

Kinnie Wagner, once called the fastest gun in the South, forced Jack Hathcock to return his money after one of Hathcock's floozies robbed him on the dance floor.

Kinnie Wagner had killed his first man, a deputy sheriff in Greene County, Mississippi, on Christmas Eve 1924. The deputy was attempting to question him about a robbery.

Wagner skedaddled to East Tennessee, where friends and relatives kept him hidden for four months. Then, during a family picnic on the banks of the Holston River in Kingsport one Sunday afternoon, law enforcement officers opened fire on him. During the shoot-out, Wagner killed a Sullivan County deputy sheriff and a city policeman. Another deputy was seriously wounded.

Wagner, who escaped unharmed, surrendered the next day. He later stood trial at the Sullivan County Courthouse in Blountville, was found guilty of murder, and was sentenced to die in the Tennessee electric chair.

In his court appeals, Wagner claimed that the law officers had attacked without warning, forcing him to fire in self-defense. He won a new trial but escaped before a new court date could be set.

Wagner showed up in Texarkana, Arkansas, where two brothers provoked him into a gunfight. He killed them both. Once again he surrendered to the authorities.

Arkansas turned him over to Mississippi officials. He was tried and convicted of murdering the Greene County deputy and sentenced to life in the prison at Parchman. Murder charges were also still pending against him in Arkansas and Tennessee.

Not only was Kinnie Wagner a deadly shot with a gun, but he was also an escape artist. Prior to his visit to the Forty-Five Grill, he had fled Parchman custody three different times.

Wagner soon forgot his "social call" at the Forty-Five Grill, but Jack Hathcock never did. Months later, he was still talking about it. "I'll never forget how close we come to the undertaker wipin' our asses that night Kinnie Wagner was here. If we'd jumped on him, he'd have shot us like he'd shoot fish in a rain barrel," Hathcock told Pee Wee Walker.

"You ain't shittin'! He's faster than greased lightnin' with a gun," remarked Walker.

CHAPTER FIVE

It was not yet dark when Warren Ingle left the Forty-Five Grill. He waited for an empty log truck to pass, then crossed U.S. 45 to the Plantation Club.

Ingle, a thirty-eight-year-old carpenter from Ramer, Tennessee, could not recall when he had been happier. He had just won five hundred dollars rolling high dice, and he could not believe his luck. Usually Jack Hathcock did not allow big winners to leave the Forty-Five Grill trouble-free.

Ingle thought that February 16, 1954, would be a date he would long remember. Instead, it would be the shortest day of his life.

He entered the Plantation Club, a large, white wood-framed building. Foot-high black letters across the front, just below the overhang of the flat roof, identified the joint.

Inside the club, owner W. O. Hathcock, Jr., was behind the bar. His wife, Larice, and Dewitt Curtis, a professional gambler, sat at a nearby table. Two women named Betty Jean and Oneida selected and punched numbers at the jukebox. Howard Carroll, one of the Forty-Five Grill flunkies, sat alone with a bottle.

Hathcock, twenty-four, husky, just under six feet with slicked-back dark hair, was tough when the odds were in his favor. He had a "bash 'em in the head from behind" reputation.

Larice, near the same age as her husband, had shoulder-length black hair. She was attractive in spite of her habit of wearing too much cheap makeup. A couple of years earlier, she had been married to a state-line gambler named Hershel Roberts.

"Give me a half-pint of Old Crow," said Ingle as he laid a twenty dollar bill on the bar.

Hathcock reached under the counter, retrieved a bottle of whiskey, and handed it to Ingle. Then he gave his customer eight dollars change.

"Whiskey gone up?" asked Ingle.

"Nope. Still two dollars a half-pint."

The carpenter, who had been drinking liquor most of the day, bristled with anger. "I gave you a twenty."

"Like hell you did. You gave me a ten."

Ingle leaned across the bar. "You crooked sonofabitch! I want my money! You Hathcocks are always tryin' to fuck somebody around," he snorted.

"Get your ass out of here! Right now!" Hathcock yelled as he rushed from behind the bar with a .38-caliber pistol in his right hand.

"You gonna throw me out 'cause I don't like you stealin' my money? I ain't done nothin' to nobody," Ingle protested.

"Shut your damned mouth and get out!" Hathcock hollered. He jammed the pistol barrel into Ingle's back, marched him to the door, jerked it open, and forced him outside. "Get off my property! And don't ever come back!" the bar owner ordered as he recklessly fired off a shot. The bullet plowed into the ground.

Ingle, his senses numbed by alcohol, refused to run. He sauntered toward the highway. Hathcock fired again. This time the slug tore into Ingle's right side, knocking him down. He struggled to his feet and staggered forward before collapsing halfway between the honky-tonk and U.S. 45.

W. O. Hathcock watched Ingle fall the second time. When he was convinced that the man was either dead or near death, he went back into the club. He was extremely calm as he picked up the telephone and dialed the Alcorn County sheriff's office.

Deputy C. L. Wilhite answered the phone. "Sheriff's office. Wilhite."

"This is W. O. Hathcock at the Plantation Club. You'd better come on out. I just had to shoot a man."

The deputy dispatched a McPeters Funeral Home ambulance to the scene. Ingle died shortly after his arrival at

Community Hospital in Corinth. Emergency room doctors said that Warren Ingle bled to death after the bullet crashed into his chest and severed a major heart artery.

Deputies Wilhite and Tom Nelson checked on Ingle's condition at the hospital before going to the Plantation. When they arrived at the club about an hour later, they found Hathcock in his living quarters behind the dance hall. He displayed no remorse and acted as if he were waiting for supper to be served.

Hathcock admitted that he had shot Ingle. "I had to shoot him. He was tryin' to cut me to pieces with a knife."

The club owner, who was wearing a brown windbreaker, pointed to a slash across the front of it. He also had a bandage on his upper left arm. He claimed the dressing covered a wound that had required nine stitches.

"Warren Ingle is dead. He died right after he got to the hospital," said Wilhite.

The unconcerned expression on Hathcock's face did not change. "I told you I had to shoot him. He was tryin' to cut me up like a butcher slaughters a hog. Right after it happened, I went straight to Dr. Frank Davis's office in Corinth and got sewed up. I was bleedin' somethin' awful," Hathcock whined.

He received no sympathy from the deputies. "You're going to have to come with us, W. O. You're under arrest for murder," said Wilhite. Hathcock was handcuffed and led to a patrol car.

He was taken before Peace Justice Lyle Taylor. The accused murderer was released on five thousand dollars bond, and a preliminary hearing date was set for February 23, 1954.

Sheriff Bobby Phillips and County Attorney N. S. Sweat, Jr., conducted an in-depth investigation of the slaying. One eyewitness agreed to talk after being assured his name would not be disclosed. He told Phillips and Sweat that Hathcock's self-defense claim had been hatched on the spot following Ingle's killing. The man quoted Hathcock as saying, "Well, I'm into it now! I've got to get set." He explained that the club owner then slipped a knife from his pants pocket and slashed himself with it.

The officials knew they could not use their witness's testimony in court. They had agreed to keep his identity cloaked in secrecy. But at least they knew the other side of the murder story.

W. O. Hathcock, Jr., stuck to his self-defense claim. His wife verified it. Dewitt Curtis maintained that he also saw Ingle trying to "carve W. O. up" with the knife. Denying that he still worked at the Plantation Club, Curtis, a Hathcock employee, said he had quit and was planning to "make a crop" that year.

The other two witnesses, Betty Jean and Oneida, told the sheriff and the county attorney that they did not see a knife in Ingle's possession while he was in the club or outside before the shooting.

More than two hundred persons attended Hathcock's two-hour, twenty-minute preliminary hearing. Peace Justice Taylor called the court to order, and County Attorney Sweat wasted no time getting down to business. He summoned the accused slayer to the witness stand. "Do you always carry a gun, Mr. Hathcock?"

"Only when I'm at the place. You never can tell when you'll need one."

"Where do you keep it?"

"In my pocket. No use to have a pistol if it ain't handy when you need it."

Sweat studied the notes that he had scribbled on a yellow legal pad he held in his right hand. "Now, Mr. Hathcock. Isn't it a fact that Warren Ingle never even had a knife, that you fabricated the self-defense story to save your own neck?"

"No, that isn't true. He tried to butcher me like a hog. I had to shoot him to save my life," Hathcock insisted.

"How many times did you shoot Warren Ingle?" asked Sweat.

"Once. I shot in the ground the first time to try and scare him. But he kept comin' at me with that knife. I had to shoot him."

Hathcock testified that he had thrown Ingle out of the Plantation Club earlier that day for fighting with three other men. He denied selling him a half-pint of whiskey. He said the argument erupted when he asked Ingle to leave when he came into the club the second time.

On the witness stand, Betty Jean and Oneida both testified that they did not know what had sparked the disagreement between Hathcock and Ingle. They said the first time they really noticed Ingle was when Hathcock had a pistol stuck in his back and was ordering him to leave the club. Both women declared that the murder victim did not have a weapon.

After hearing all the evidence, Peace Justice Lyle Taylor bound the case over to the Alcorn County grand jury. W. O. Hathcock, Jr., was later indicted for murder.

Meanwhile, another Hathcock was wearing a good Samaritan robe. Louise Hathcock, who could kill in cold blood one day and lend a helping hand to the needy the next, was displaying her charitable colors.

Her brother, William Anderson, who had been hospitalized with pneumonia in Corinth's Community Hospital, was directly across the hall from nine-year-old Frankie Jo Bingham. The youngster was confined with yellow jaundice.

Frankie Jo's parents, Grady and Elsie Bingham, knew of Louise Hathcock only by reputation. They had long heard about the Hathcocks' lawless escapades, but they had never met Louise before their daughter's short hospital confinement.

Grady Bingham, who would become sheriff of Alcorn County fourteen years later, was then working for a natural gas company in Corinth. In addition to his wife and himself, he had three daughters to support.

Late one evening, Frankie Jo's crying prompted Louise Hathcock to visit the small girl's room. "That child needs special care!" she declared. "She needs to be taken to a doctor in Memphis! I've got a brand-new Cadillac outside and plenty of money to cover expenses. I want you to take my car and money and carry your daughter to Memphis right now."

Grady moved closer to Frankie Jo's bedside, smoothing a wrinkle in the sheet with his hand. "We really appreciate your concern for our little girl, Mrs. Hathcock. But our doctor says Frankie Jo will be fine again very soon."

"I don't care what your doctor says. Your child needs a specialist now! You need to take her to Memphis right away."

Bingham rubbed his chin with his hand. "Believe me, Mrs. Hathcock, we do sincerely appreciate you offering to help us. It's mighty kind of you. But we'll just wait for now and take our doctor's advice. I've got a car. It's certainly not a new one, but I think it would make the trip to Memphis. And I got some money. My wife and I certainly appreciate your generous offer though."

Disappointment settled on Louise Hathcock's face. "I think you're makin' a big mistake, but it's your decision. If you change your mind or if I can be of any help to you, please don't hesitate to call on me."

Louise abruptly left the room.

Frankie Jo Bingham fully recovered from yellow jaundice without leaving Community Hospital.

Weeks later, when Louise Hathcock answered the telephone in her Corinth home, she was greeted by undertaker Bill McPeters. "Louise, this is Bill. How are you doing this morning?"

"I've felt better. Had a big night at the club. My ass is draggin'."

"You can't complain when the greenbacks are rolling in."

"I heard that."

"Louise, one of the neighbors lost everything in a house fire last night. I was wondering if you could help out."

"Sure. Be glad to. How much you givin', Bill?"

"I'm going to let them have a couple of hundred."

"Then I'll give 'em five hundred."

Louise Hathcock often donated money to worthy causes. She thought of herself as a female Robin Hood; but unlike the folk hero, she not only robbed the rich, she also bilked the poor. All persons, whether they had pockets full of cash or just their weekly wages, were open game when Louise decided to zero in on them at the Forty-Five Grill.

It would have been easier to find a black man at a Ku Klux Klan rally than to find the Hathcock name missing from the weekly police blotter.

On October 20, 1954, the Forty-Five Grill became the focus of a murder investigation. Although Jack Hathcock

had instigated the crime, h
ecution.

One of his henchmen, Jo
former beer-joint owner Ed
and his son attempted to ent
the state-line mob played its
Defense."

Fowlkes told investigators
George forced him to trigger
Until it had been recently level
ated a dive on Boneyard Roa
"Towhead" White, a deserter fro
Forty-Five Grill employee, sup ....kes's self-de-
fense story.

Fowlkes was char
three thousand d
later ruled th

The de
abou
li

George died at Corinth's Community Hospital from shock and the excessive loss of blood caused by massive gunshot wounds. There were six wounds in his right shoulder, and his legs had been peppered with buckshot.

Both Fowlkes and White claimed that George had parked his pickup truck in front of the restaurant door and climbed out, carrying a pistol in his right hand. They said that George's son was close on his heels. According to them, when Fowlkes blasted Ed George with buckshot, the younger George scooped up the pistol and ran away.

The son, E. W. George, told officials that his father was unarmed when they arrived at the Forty-Five Grill. He said Fowlkes opened fire on his daddy the second he stepped from the truck.

According to young George, he and his father had come to the Forty-Five to "mend fences." The shooting was the climax of the previous night's scrap between the Georges and Jack Hathcock, Fowlkes, and White. The Georges had gone into the dance hall section of the Grill, and trouble immediately broke out among them. The thugs severely beat the younger George, slapped the "ole man" around some, and then threw them out the back door. Less than thirty minutes later, father and son returned and fired several shots into the building from the outside.

Jack Hathcock instructed Fowlkes and White to "shoot the Georges on sight" if they ever came back to the Forty-Five Grill.

...ged with manslaughter and released on ...llars bond. The Alcorn County grand jury ...t he had killed Ed George in self-defense.

...ent folks of Alcorn County were becoming outraged ...t their elected officials' inability to control the state-...e corruption. They demanded more action and less talk. Knowing the heat had been turned up, Jack Hathcock decided to smother the red-hot blaze with a blanket of greenbacks.

The county Junior Chamber of Commerce was preparing to sponsor a "Hillbilly Jamboree" at the courthouse in Corinth on January 17, 1955. Hathcock knew that all the civic leaders—big and small—were pushing the event to raise funds for a children's playground. Past experiences had taught him that money could instantly change the spots on a political leopard, so he donated eight hundred dollars to the playground project. He even took his seven-year-old adopted daughter, Jeanette Susan, to the country music shindig.

A young Elvis Presley appeared on the Corinth show, but he was overshadowed by headliners Bob Neal, a popular Memphis radio personality, and "Louisiana Hayride" stars Jim Ed and Maxine Brown. Hundreds of people gathered at the Alcorn County Courthouse to enjoy the music. Although Elvis Presley was being promoted as "one of the fastest-rising young stars in the nation," he attracted little attention. Most folks had flocked to the jamboree to see established entertainers Neal and the Browns perform in the flesh.

Apparently Jack Hathcock's strategy worked. The stateline flames died as quickly as they had roared to life.

The murder trial of W. O. Hathcock, Jr., dominated the courthouse scene on January 28, 1955. Half of the day was spent selecting a jury. The only witness was Dr. Frank Davis, who testified that he had treated Hathcock for knife wounds following Ingle's fatal shooting on February 16, 1954.

N. S. Sweat, Jr., the county attorney, decided that the doctor's testimony was too stout to dilute. During pre-trial questioning, the physician had hinted that Hathcock's wounds might have been self-inflicted, but now he made it clear that "in his professional opinion" someone else had knifed the Plantation Club owner. Sweat knew that a local doctor's word carried much weight with members of the jury, especially those who depended on him for their own medical advice.

The county attorney asked Judge Raymond Jarvis to dismiss the murder charges against Hathcock. He advised that the state of Mississippi did not have enough solid evidence to offset the nightclub owner's claim that he had fired his .38-caliber Smith & Wesson in self-defense.

Two elderly farmers, wearing soiled felt hats and new bibbed overalls, were "hot under the collar" when they left the courthouse. "Tryin' to hem them Hathcocks up is like tryin' to catch a greased pig and hold it. For some reason, the law can never get enough evidence to send any of 'em to the pen," one of them complained.

"Them Hathcocks got enough money to choke a horse. Course, they stole it all, but they got it just the same. When any of 'em gets their ass in a crack, they drop a bundle of cash in the right places and keep on operatin' full blast," replied the other farmer.

CHAPTER SIX

Rain hammered the windows. Now and then thunderbolts shook the entire Forty-Five Grill. Lights weakened, then regained their strength.

Jack Hathcock stood at the front door watching the rain pelt the glass, flinching each time the lightning flashed. "It's comin' a Noah's flood out there. Been rainin' all damned day and half the night. Sure plays hell with business. Keeps everybody run off," he complained.

Everett "Pee Wee" Walker and Nancy Harris, a fifteen-year-old runaway from Indiana, were the only other people in the restaurant. "Yeah. It's nasty outside. Gonna be a real slow night," Walker answered. He was sitting with the teenage girl at a table near the door.

Nancy, who had been at the Forty-Five Grill for almost two months, earned her keep by peddling sex. She looked much older than she was. Attractive and well built, with long black hair, she was extremely popular with the whorechasers. Hathcock knew that Nancy Harris was a runaway, but he planned to let her stay around as long as she continued to make him money.

Walker, short and slim with dark brown, curly hair, was thirty years old. He was a ladies' man, and he had a lofty personality. A long-time associate of Jack Hathcock, he was a charter member of the state-line mob.

More money-hungry than Silas Marner himself, Hathcock was miserable when the greenbacks were not rolling in. He stared at the rain and thought about the time wet weather wiped out his daddy's cotton crop. Will Hathcock, a staunch unbeliever, had climbed a tall oak tree and cursed God. Jack considered repeating his father's blasphemous ritual.

"Wonder if anybody's over in the dance hall? Think I'll go check it out," sighed Walker as he scooted his chair back from the table. "You want to come along, Nancy?"

The girl, who was nursing a half-pint of Yellowstone, shook her head. "No. I'll just stay here and enjoy my booze. But if you find a horny dude over there with a lot of cash, call me," she smiled.

"Wasn't a handful over there awhile ago. Doubt if anybody else has come in. Keeps rainin' like a cow pissin' on a flat rock. Fuck this weather," growled Hathcock.

There were only twenty-three customers in the dance hall. The usual Thursday night crowd consisted of seventy to eighty.

As he entered the ballroom, Walker bumped into an old friend.

"Hey, Pee Wee. How you doin', man?"

"Doin' fine, Cletus. Haven't seen you in a month of Sundays. How'd your cotton crop turn out this year?"

"Real good. Cotton's up, too. Fellow sold the first bale of the season the other day. Lowe Brothers bought it and paid thirty-six cents a pound. The bale weighed 435 pounds."

"Maybe I'd better start growin' cotton. Good to see you again, Cletus. I'll catch you later," grinned Walker as he headed toward Louise Hathcock.

She was standing in a haze of cigarette and cigar smoke next to a table in the far corner. There Bobby Floyd was hustling a couple of guys with the three-card-monte trick. Floyd, short and medium built, was also a state-line veteran. He specialized in cards and dice.

Walker motioned Louise away from the table.

"Seen anybody with a large roll of dough yet?" he asked.

"No. It's real slim pickin's tonight. Damned weather!" she frowned.

"That's right. Not many here. But you never can tell. One of 'em might have a roll on him," Walker smiled.

Lightning dimmed the lights again. "Damn. It's already dark in here, and when the lights flicker off, it blinds you," Louise complained.

Suddenly an argument erupted at a dice table in the rear of the dance hall. Louise and Pee Wee rushed to the scene.

Hershel Roberts, a real gambling pro, was running the game. The dice table was rigged with electronic devices that allowed the "house man" remote control of the roll of the cubes.

"This game is as crooked as a barrel of snakes. I saw them dice stop all of a sudden on craps. This damned table is wired," a young, redheaded man protested. Roberts blocked his attempt to kneel down and inspect the under-side of the table.

"Hey! Get your ass outta here! You don't come in here and accuse us of cheatin'!" Louise shouted.

"Look. This table is rigged. I saw the dice just freeze on the board. Give my $163 back, and I'll leave. No questions asked."

"You're gonna leave all right—face first!" Louise threat-ened.

Walker snatched the man away from the table. When he resisted, Louise Hathcock slammed him in the head with her ball peen hammer. Pee Wee led the stunned dice player to the back door.

"The bastard still owes us money. He didn't pay up after he lost that last roll of the dice," snapped Roberts.

Louise quickly rifled through the young man's pockets and billfold. She crammed $157 into her apron pocket, then opened the door. The man was dazed, but he was still on his feet. Walker bashed the "gambler" in the head a couple of times with a .38-caliber pistol.

"Hurry up, Pee Wee. Throw the sonofabitch outside. He's bleedin' all over the floor," Louise scoffed.

Walker and Roberts threw the unconscious "customer" out into the cold, rain-swept night.

When the victim recovered, he hurriedly left the state line for his home in Florence, Alabama. He did not want to hassle with the thugs in court or anywhere else.

In mid-1955 numerous complaints about the criminal wrongdoing at the Forty-Five Grill were addressed to Gov-ernor Hugh White at the state capitol in Jackson, Mis-sissippi. After several meetings with his attorney general, the governor ordered the highway patrol to crack down on the roadhouse.

Jack Hathcock, a generous contributor to various political war chests, pulled a few strings. The governor agreed to back off after Hathcock promised to remove the "Country Ham" road signs and strictly enforce the no-gambling rule.

Alcorn County Attorney N. S. Sweat, Jr., had also received a stack of accusations against the Forty-Five Grill. He said his office files were bulging with reports from tourists who claimed they had been fleeced by the Hathcock gang.

"You may have conned the governor and his staff into swallowing your cock-and-bull story about going straight, but you're not conning me," Sweat warned Hathcock. "They don't know you at the state capitol like I know you. They don't know you're so damned crooked the undertaker will have to screw you into the ground.

"But let me tell you something, Hathcock. You'd better not even get caught selling Bibles without a license. It's just a matter of time before I close down the Forty-Five Grill," vowed Sweat.

The sands in the 1955 hourglass emptied before Sweat could accomplish his goal. But on January 1, 1956, a new slate of Alcorn County law enforcement officials swore to continue the war on the state-line hoodlums.

CHAPTER SEVEN

The changing of the guard at the Alcorn County court-house brought fresh ideas on how to put the lid on corruption at the state line. The new officials had been elected on old promises their forerunners had found it impossible to keep.

Sheriff Lyle Taylor, one of the new public servants, had an edge on his recently elected colleagues. During his past four years as a justice of the peace, Taylor had handled countless cases involving Jack Hathcock and other state-line thugs. He was familiar with their criminal tactics.

Taylor had often flinched with disgust when he was forced to free the hoodlums due to weak evidence or because they had paid off key witnesses. Now, as sheriff, he vowed that he would gather unimpeachable evidence and close down their lawless operations.

In his late fifties with a paunchy midsection, Taylor stood just under five feet ten inches. His no-nonsense personality commanded respect. He wore a narrow-brimmed hat to hide his baldness, and his usual attire was a white shirt, a dark tie, black pants, and a brown, waist-length sports jacket.

From day one, the sheriff and his deputies—R. C. McNair, Earl Mills, Robert Burns, and Grady Bingham— kept their fingers on the state-line pulse beat.

Right off the bat, they uncovered a large cache of whiskey hidden in a sprawling honeysuckle patch just inside the Mississippi line. Taylor knew that the 206 half-pints of liquor belonged to Jack Hathcock, but he could not prove ownership.

Carl Douglas "Towhead" White arrived in Alcorn County in 1953, vowing to become the Al Capone of the South. Before his death in 1969, he had been labeled by the FBI as one of the most dangerous criminals in the United States.

Near the middle of January 1956 a new face—new to the sheriff and his deputies, at least—surfaced at the Forty-Five Grill. The lawmen, for the first time, rubbed shoulders with Carl Douglas "Towhead" White.

Actually, White was no stranger to the area. He had worked at the roadhouse in 1953 while he was on the run from the air force. After a brief stay with the "men in blue," he had gone A.W.O.L., and the next year, while he was still absent without leave from the air force, he enlisted in the army.

White signed up for military duty both times in Jackson, Mississippi, and both times he lied about his age. He was fifteen the first time and sixteen the second, but each time he swore he was three years older.

Now, with a dishonorable discharge in his growing police files, Towhead White was back at the state line. The eighteen-year-old outlaw was planning to make Alcorn County his permanent home.

As the officers were leaving the Forty-Five Grill, Grady Bingham nudged Sheriff Taylor in the ribs with his elbow. "We're going to have to keep a close eye on that bastard named White, Sheriff. I'll bet he'd steal the nickels from a dead man's eyes."

"Yeah. He seems like a smooth operator. Slick tongued. Nice lookin'. Bet he's never done an honest day's work in his life," said Taylor. The lawmen soon learned that their hasty evaluation of White was correct.

On January 20, 1956, Deputies Grady Bingham and Robert Burns arrested White for assault and battery. A local sailor, home on furlough from the Memphis Naval Air Station in Millington, Tennessee, had filed the charges. He said White attacked him on U.S. 45 South in Corinth after the two of them left a dive, but he refused to give Bingham and Burns detailed information about the assault.

The sailor was hospitalized with a broken right ankle, severe head injuries, and deep facial cuts. White sent word to him that amnesia was his only hope of "remaining healthy" after his hospital release. The sailor dropped the charges against the young thug.

Less than a week later, Bingham received a complaint that Towhead White was bootlegging whiskey from his rented house near the city cemetery in Corinth. After discussing the matter with Sheriff Taylor, Bingham obtained a search warrant for White's house. It was as dry as a powder keg. The hoodlum had hidden his liquor in a weed-choked field across the road from his residence.

White's booze saga continued.

On February 13, 1956, Bingham and Deputy Robert Burns stopped the gangster's beige-colored 1954 Oldsmobile on U.S. 72 near Corinth. White was charged with exceeding the speed limit and having no driver's license.

A passenger in White's car, Jerry Eubanks, was arrested for possessing five half-pints of whiskey. The liquor actually belonged to White, but Eubanks claimed ownership.

Peace Justice Homer "Pete" Richardson fined the men one hundred dollars each.

The following Saturday morning, Bingham was driving on a side road west of Corinth when he spotted a fresh pile of garbage in an open field. He stopped to investigate, and while prowling through the trash, he found an envelope addressed to Towhead White. Then he saw the end of a cardboard box. It was a full case of Old Charter whiskey.

The deputy loaded the booze into the patrol car. White, he thought, was pretty smooth. He had dumped the garbage in the field and stashed his liquor in it. If the law showed up while he was there, he would claim he was only discarding trash. White would swear that he knew nothing about the letter with his name on it or who owned the whiskey, and the evidence against him would never stand up in court.

"That damned Towhead White is a shifty bastard. He's hard to catch with the goods on him," Bingham told his boss.

"Yeah. He's slicker than owl shit. But we'll nail his ass. Just have to keep on top of him," the sheriff responded.

Towhead White was quickly getting his foot in the state-line door, but he was not yet a major problem. Jack Hathcock and his main sidekick, Everett "Pee Wee" Walker, were still the kingpins of the crime-infested border.

Sheriff Taylor and his deputies burned up more than their share of county gasoline making trips to the state line. Taylor demanded that every complaint about the Hathcock gang be promptly investigated.

One evening, Bingham parked his black Ford cruiser in front of the Alcorn County Jail. Before he could climb from the car, a tall, muscular man in his early twenties placed his hand on the opened door.

"You the sheriff? I just been robbed of fifty dollars at a joint called the Forty-Five Grill."

"No, sir, I'm not the sheriff. Don't think he's around right now."

The man stepped back from the car, and Bingham got out. "Do you know who robbed you?" asked the deputy.

"Some punk called Pee Wee. He's about the size of a piss ant."

"That's Pee Wee Walker. Him and the Hathcocks are professional thieves. You wanna sign a warrant?"

"Hell, yes! That little sonofabitch cheated me blind. Kept on palmin' the dice. When I caught him red-handed, I asked for my money back. Then him and two other goons throwed me out."

"You shouldn't have been gamblin' out there. It's against the law to shoot dice for money," said Bingham.

"There wasn't any gambling to it. It's not gambling when you don't have a chance to win in the first place. It was pure stealing," the man insisted.

"I guess you're right. That damned bunch at the state line call it gamblin', but like you said, it's really robbery in disguise," agreed the deputy. "What's your name anyway?"

"Josh Turner. I live in Muscle Shoals, Alabama."

After obtaining a warrant for Walker's arrest, Bingham asked Deputy Robert Burns to ride with him to the Forty-Five Grill. Turner was instructed to remain at the jail until the deputies returned.

Less than thirty minutes later, Bingham and Burns were back at the jail with Walker in custody. Before anyone could get out of the sheriff's cruiser, Jack and Louise Hathcock arrived in her new Cadillac.

The deputies ignored the Hathcocks as they hustled Walker inside to a small room next to Sheriff Taylor's office. The hoodlum came face to face with his accuser. "That's him! That's the bastard who took my money," Turner snapped.

"Yore a damn liar! I ain't never seen you before," bristled Walker.

Jack and Louise had hurried into the office and were standing behind their associate.

"You're real tough when you got a couple of other thugs with you. If it was all right with the law, I'd take you outside and whip your ass," Turner threatened.

Both Bingham and Burns thought Turner had an excellent idea. They figured the Alabama man, who looked like a pro boxer, could give "ole Pee Wee" a good dose of his own medicine. "It's fine with us. Take him outside," grinned Bingham.

Jack Hathcock interrupted. "Go on out there, Pee Wee, and beat hell outta the motherfucker. Teach him he can't come up here and tell bald-faced lies on us."

Bingham moved next to Hathcock. "You yellow-bellied bastard! If you're so brave, why don't you whip somebody?"

Hathcock looked like a scrawny kid collared by the school bully. His mouth closed faster than a mouse-triggered trap.

The deputies followed Walker and Turner outside with the Hathcocks close on their heels.

A narrow gravel road ran between the old two-story brick jail building and a set of railroad tracks. Without warning, Turner smashed Walker in the jaw with a solid right punch. The thug sprawled to the gravel. His assailant pounced on him with catlike quickness. Turner slammed Walker's head back and forth on the crushed rocks.

Louise Hathcock rushed to Walker's rescue, kicking Turner in the head several times with her spiked-heel shoes.

Bingham spun her around.

"Get yore hands offa me! Yore messin' with somebody now who'll fight hell outta you," Louise warned the deputy.

"Let me tell you somethin', bitch! I'll knock your ass plumb across them railroad tracks over there! I'd rather hit you than any man I ever saw!" snorted Bingham. His words left the female outlaw tongue-tied.

Finally, Pee Wee Walker ran up the white flag. Turner quickly scrambled to his feet while Louise pulled the battered hoodlum up from the gravel.

"You gave that bastard a good ass-whippin'," smiled Bingham. "He needed it real bad.

"Let me see if I can save you a trip back here. Maybe I can get Judge Richardson to come over, and we can settle this case tonight. Then you won't have to drive back from Alabama for a hearing."

Bingham persuaded Peace Justice Homer Richardson to come to the jail. After listening to both sides of the story, Richardson found Walker guilty of theft. He fined the gangster $250 and forced him to repay the $50 he had stolen from Turner.

A few days later, Sheriff Lyle Taylor received a complaint from a Memphis man charging Louise Hathcock with swiping four hundred dollars from him. The oil company salesman said the woman bandit had stolen his billfold while they were dancing at the Forty-Five Grill. Taylor told Grady Bingham to obtain a robbery warrant and arrest Louise.

Bingham wasted a trip to the state line, but he found Louise Hathcock at her home on Proper Street in Corinth.

The Hathcock dwelling was a large, expensive brick structure trimmed with fieldstone. The yard was immaculate.

The deputy rapped on the door, and Louise, dressed in a powder-blue nightgown, peeked out through a small glass in the wooden barrier. She cracked the door open. "What do you want, Bingham? It's not even nine o'clock yet."

"Got a warrant for your arrest, Louise. A Memphis fellow said you stole four hundred dollars off him."

"He's a lyin' sonofabitch! I ain't stole a penny from nobody. Every time some Tom, Dick, or Harry whines about us, you law dogs can't wait to arrest our asses."

"I'm not in the mood for any of your bullshit, Louise. You're gonna have to come with me."

Louise clearly recalled Bingham's words: "I'd rather hit you than any man I ever saw." She was convinced that he meant it.

"Could I get dressed first?"

"Yeah. But hurry up."

Louise quickly disappeared into another room.

Bingham pushed open the front door and stepped into the living room. The luxurious furniture and plush carpet made anger boil inside him. All the elegance, he thought, was the fruit of dishonesty. Decent, hard-working people existed from paycheck to paycheck while these criminals lived like kings.

Louise returned to the room wearing her customary black uniform-styled outfit. Except for the white apron, which she usually left at the dance hall, she was ready for work. "Why don't you let me follow you in my car? I'll make bond as soon as we get to Richardson's office anyway. Then I'll just drive on out to the restaurant and go to work," she smiled.

"Hell, no! You're under arrest and in my personal custody! And you're gonna stay in my personal custody until the judge turns you loose!"

"Okay. We'll do it your way. Let's go," she smirked as she followed the deputy out the door and pulled it shut behind her.

Bingham knew that Louise Hathcock would be freed within minutes after they reached Peace Justice Homer Richardson's court. The Hathcocks could make bond faster than lightning could flash. He also knew that she would never try to escape, but he wanted to inconvenience her as much as possible.

Richardson released Louise on one thousand dollars bond. A preliminary hearing was set for two weeks later. But the oil company salesman failed to show for the hearing, and the case was scrapped. Louise had paid the man six hundred dollars for his four hundred dollar loss.

Three weeks later Grady Bingham was in a truck stop west of Corinth when the salesman sauntered in. "Howdy, Deputy. Good to see you again. Everything worked out fine as frog hair with my deal at the Forty-Five Grill. Got my money back plus some extra loot for my trouble."

Disgust froze Bingham's face. He despised those who caved in to the Hathcocks. "You're as low-down as the Hathcocks are. It's people like you who keep us from runnin' all them state-line bastards off. The very idea! Takin' their bribe money! Now, you get your ass out of Alcorn County, and don't you ever let me catch you here again!" warned Bingham.

The man, caught by total surprise and left speechless, quickly exited the truck stop.

The deputy realized that he could not legally keep the salesman out of the county. Nonetheless, his blunt words gave him pleasure. He wanted everyone to know that he detested the filth at the state line and all who "kissed their asses."

CHAPTER EIGHT

$\mathbf{A}$ light drizzle was falling when Towhead White strolled through the back door of the Forty-Five Grill and seated himself at a corner table in the dance hall. Wearing a dark blue silk suit, a light gray shirt, and a red tie, he was careful not to scuff his black mirror-polished, wing-tipped shoes against a table leg.

The crowd was small, which was normal for an early Tuesday afternoon.

An eighteen-year-old waitress named Betty Jo hurried to White's table. Her auburn hair cascaded almost to her small waist, and her facial features were flawless. She could have caused a penniless man with a wealthy wife to leave home. "Wow! You gonna preach somewhere tonight? You're really dressed up!" Betty Jo laughed as she slid onto a chair next to White.

"Only if they guarantee me a lot of bread when they pass the collection plate." White slipped a half-pint of Old Charter from his back pocket and laid it on the table.

"You're either goin' partyin', or you're goin' out of town on business," Betty Jo smiled.

"Business trip."

"Where to this time?"

"Atlanta. Keep it under your hat."

When she was not waiting tables at the Forty-Five, Betty Jo worked for White as a prostitute. She had convinced the Hathcocks that "under no circumstances" would she peddle sex. Sometimes she did line the "Johns" up during work hours, but she usually made her "dates" while bar-hopping after she had pulled her shift at the Forty-Five Grill.

56

"You goin' to Atlanta by yourself?"

"No. Got a friend goin' with me. He'll be here pretty soon." White unscrewed the cap from the liquor bottle and took a drink. Then he lit a cigarette.

"You love sports, Towhead. Thought you'd be downtown for the Don Blasingame parade."

"Damn. I did want to see him. Been so busy, it slipped my mind."

Corinth merchants and civic leaders had organized a "Don Blasingame Day" parade to honor Alcorn County's first major league baseball player on this Tuesday, October 2, 1956. Blasingame had just completed his rookie season with the St. Louis Cardinals.

White's cohort wandered through the front door of the dance hall.

"There's my man. Go tell him to come over here," White told Betty Jo. She immediately jumped up, went to the front, and escorted the hoodlum to White's table.

"Betty Jo, this is Sam Grooms. We're old friends. Betty Jo here is one of my hookers."

"Damn! I'd give a hundred dollars for some of that right now," Grooms drooled.

"We ain't got time. Got to hit the road. She'll be here when we get back," White promised.

Erwin Samuel Grooms, still in his early twenties, was an expert safe burglar from Dallas, Texas. White and the safe-cracker had met while White was on the lam from the air force. The two thugs were planning to knock off the safe at a large department store in Atlanta, Georgia.

As White and Grooms were leaving the dance hall through the back door, they encountered Pee Wee Walker. "Hey, Tow. Is Jack or Louise in there? Need to see one of 'em real bad."

"Think Louise is still at home. Haven't seen Jack. He may be over in the restaurant."

Walker frowned. "Well, I just got word the damned sheriff is gonna raid this place for whiskey."

"I'm gettin' outta here now! Don't need no hassle with the law," said White as he gently pushed Grooms out the door.

It was a false alarm. Sheriff Lyle Taylor had circulated the rumors. He knew there was a leak at the courthouse, but he had been unable to locate it. Whether he found the rat hole or not, he planned to keep the "bastards" confused.

Taylor and County Attorney H. M. Ray had been gathering evidence against the Hathcock gang ever since they were sworn into office. They were determined to keep their campaign promises to "clean up" the Mississippi border.

The state-line file continued to grow. Since the murder there in 1954, the Plantation Club had calmed down. But the Forty-Five Grill was raging like a tropical storm.

On November 2, 1956, an irate gambler signed theft warrants against Jack Hathcock and Pee Wee Walker. He charged the two racketeers with swindling him in a dice game at the Forty-Five.

When Sheriff Lyle Taylor and Deputies R. C. McNair and Grady Bingham arrested Hathcock and Walker at the roadhouse, they found a .38-caliber Smith & Wesson on Hathcock. Walker was clean.

The deputies searched a back room and returned with an eight-pocket vest. Each pouch contained a half-pint of whiskey. "Whose liquor is this?" asked Bingham.

Alcorn County authorities inventory a cache of bootleg whiskey during a raid of the Forty-Five Grill. From left to right: Sheriff Lyle Taylor, County Attorney H. M. Ray, and deputy sheriffs Earl Mills, R. C. McNair, and Grady Bingham.

"Hell, how should I know?" smirked Hathcock.

The sheriff rolled his eyes in disgust. "Okay. We'll charge you both with possessing whiskey," shrugged Taylor.

"It's mine. Don't want Jack takin' the heat when he's not guilty," said Walker.

Again the sheriff rolled his eyes.

Both Hathcock and Walker were charged with operating a dice game. Hathcock was also charged with carrying a concealed weapon, and accusations of possessing whiskey for resale were tacked onto the allegations against Walker.

The hoodlums appeared before Peace Justice Buck Sorrell and were released on bonds of one thousand dollars each. Sorrell dismissed the charges on November 7, 1956.

Immediately after the cases were nullified, County Attorney H. M. Ray filed a petition in chancery court asking that the Forty-Five Grill be declared a "public nuisance." And he asked the court to close its doors.

In his legal documents to Chancellor William Inzer, Ray wrote:

> The Forty-Five Grill is a building and place wherein intoxicating liquors of all kinds and descriptions are kept and wherein intoxicating liquors of all kinds and descriptions are consumed therein in violation of the laws of the State of Mississippi and subject to abatement as a common nuisance as provided by Section 2646 of the Mississippi Code of 1942.

Ray continued:

> . . . And further prays this honorable court to enjoin the further use, occupancy, and operation of said building and place for the purpose of violating the laws of this State prohibiting intoxicating liquors.

The county attorney also asked the court to forever ban Jack Hathcock from operating a business where intoxicating beverages were kept or sold.

The ink had barely dried on the court papers when Deputy Grady Bingham received a tip about a liquor violation at the Forty-Five Grill. A search warrant for the entire building was obtained on November 24, 1956.

Sheriff Lyle Taylor and Deputies Bingham, R. C. McNair, and Earl Mills raided the Forty-Five Grill. A body search of Howard Carroll, a wino who worked for Jack Hathcock, turned up five half-pints of liquor. Hathcock did not have any contraband on him.

Acting on information from the tipster, the officers found eight cases of Missouri-taxed whiskey underneath the floor in a back bedroom. The liquor, stashed inside Domino sugar sacks, could be reached only through a trapdoor hidden under a rug beneath a dresser.

Across the highway from the dive, Taylor uncovered twenty additional half-pints of booze concealed in the framework of a V-shaped road sign. Now painted solid white, the billboard had advertised country ham, red-eye gravy, and homemade biscuits.

Jack Hathcock and Howard Carroll were arrested and charged with keeping whiskey for resale. Each man posted a one thousand dollar bond.

When questioned by the sheriff and the county attorney, Carroll denied ownership of the five half-pints found on him. "Pee Wee Walker gave that booze to me to sell. It belonged to him or Jack. Maybe it belonged to both of 'em. I don't know."

The officials knew that Carroll was only a pawn in Hathcock's hands, but they also knew that, with a little bluffing, he could be persuaded to talk. "You don't want to pay a big fine and go to jail for something Hathcock and Walker did, do you?" asked Taylor.

Ray interrupted. "And this is as serious as a heart attack this time. I filed papers in chancery court prohibiting anyone from possessing or selling whiskey at the Forty-Five Grill. The judge will throw the book at anybody who violates that court order."

The county attorney failed to tell Carroll that Chancellor Inzer had not yet ruled on his petition. The maneuver worked.

"I'll tell you the whole story," promised Carroll. "I been sellin' whiskey for Jack and Pee Wee for a long time. I don't know where they keep it. The only place I know about is that sign across the highway.

"They pay me fifteen dollars a week and give me a place

to sleep and my grub. Most of the time I even have to buy my own booze from 'em.

"Pee Wee wakes me up when he leaves the club, usually around three-thirty in the mornin'. He leaves me twelve or fourteen half-pints to sell. If I run out, I can go across the highway to that V-shaped sign and get some more.

"I run the place every day until about two in the afternoon when Jack or Louise or Pee Wee comes back to work. Course, any of 'em is likely to come in at any time of the day," said Carroll.

The charges against Howard Carroll were dropped. Later, Jack Hathcock was fined one hundred dollars by Peace Justice Buck Sorrell for possessing illegal whiskey.

Although Sorrell had handed Hathcock only a token fine, Taylor and Ray knew that they had the state-line mobster on the ropes. Hathcock knew it, too.

He moved quickly to head off the court order that would shut down his illegal operations. Because he could not afford to be forever barred from running a place where intoxicating beverages were sold, he devised a scheme that would shred his pending court documents.

Alcorn County Sheriff Lyle Taylor stands beside the V-shaped sign where Jack Hathcock stashed his bootleg whiskey.

Hathcock announced that Frank Hughes, an automobile dealer, had purchased the Forty-Five Grill property for $15,000. The story even ran on the front page of the *Daily Corinthian*.

Although Jack and Louise had legally conveyed the property to their adopted daughter, Jeanette Susan Hathcock, on September 3, 1954, Jack still controlled the real estate. He took the necessary measures to make the sale.

Actually, Hathcock had no intention of relinquishing the property. He was already planning to destroy the Forty-Five Grill, thus causing Hughes to want to sell the remaining unimproved plot of land back to him at a bargain basement price.

Frank Hughes had no idea that Hathcock had engineered a scam to dupe the authorities. Hughes even nailed the doors of the old club shut and padlocked them. Then he said the building would be remodeled and turned into a truck stop.

Hathcock had to convince the county attorney that the roadhouse would never again be the hallmark of crime. He was sure that Ray would drop the court petition if he really believed that was the case.

Jack Hathcock put the wheels into motion to burn the restaurant and dance hall to the ground. He could always construct a new building, but if he ever lost his licenses to operate a business, he could never regain them.

Just after sundown on Christmas Day 1956, the Forty-Five Grill burst into flames. When the heat and smoke had faded into the cold winter air, only ashes and charred metal testified to the fact that the notorious roadhouse had once sat on that spot.

Hathcock's scheme worked. The county attorney filed a motion to dismiss the petition to snatch the hoodlum's liquor privileges. Chancellor William Inzer approved H. M. Ray's motion for dismissal on the grounds that the property had been sold by Hathcock and had since been destroyed by fire.

Jack Hathcock felt that he was even more foxy than Civil War General Nathan Bedford Forrest had been. Relishing his victory, Hathcock purchased the land back from Hughes "for a song" and immediately launched plans to build a new restaurant and motel on the property where his old establishment had burned.

CHAPTER NINE

The night air was crisp. A late evening mist had changed to a slow-falling rain. Fog ascended from the nearby swampy bottoms and crept across the landscape.

Buford Pusser braked his 1950 Chevrolet in the graveled parking lot of the Plantation Club. He switched off the lights and climbed out.

Pusser, an ex-Marine from Adamsville, Tennessee, had recently been released from Baptist Hospital in Memphis. He had suffered a broken back when a car driven by a friend was forced from the highway. The accident had occurred only days after his discharge from the Marine Corps.

February 1957 was quickly evaporating. The doctor had said Pusser could seek employment after the first of March, and this would be his last fling before he devoted himself full-time to job hunting.

Pusser had last journeyed to the state line when he was a seventeen-year-old high school student. He would never forget the experience.

He had watched Louise Hathcock beat a sailor to death with a hammer. He could still see the lifeless body of the uniformed Navy man sprawled on the floor. And Louise's cruel smile. What disturbed him most was the fact that Louise Hathcock had gotten off scot-free.

He wondered why he had even wanted to come here again. Then he admitted to himself that he, like the others there that night, had been lured to the strip by a desire for excitement that overshadowed his better judgment.

Pusser ran his hands through his rain-dampened crew cut, then entered the club.

A slender waitress in a skintight dress greeted him. "Want a table?"

"I'd appreciate one."

"Follow me."

He watched the easy play of her hips against the clinging fabric as the waitress wove through the crowd to a table near the back. He liked what he saw. He ordered gin and soda. From a back room, he heard loud noises mixed with the clatter of dice.

Pusser still had about seventy-five dollars of his mustering-out pay from the Marines. He toyed with the idea of trying to increase the amount.

"Wonder if I could get in the game back there?" he asked the waitress as he ordered another drink.

She looked at the ex-Marine and saw a big country boy trying to butcher one last "fatted calf" before spring plowing began. The boys in the back would welcome some new money in the game. "Wait a minute. I'll find out."

The waitress rapped softly on the door of the room and was let in. In a few minutes she returned and told Pusser he had been cleared.

"Thanks," he smiled as he left his drink on the table and passed through the door she was holding open.

The room was well lighted, crowded, and smoky, and a poker game was in full swing at a table next to one wall. In the middle, several men were gathered around a long, narrow dice table.

"What's your game, big boy? Dice or cards?"

Pusser stood six feet, six inches and had weighed 250 before the hospital stay trimmed 15 pounds from his muscular frame. He was nineteen years old.

"Dice," he answered, then moved closer to the table, which was covered with one- and five-dollar bills. There were even a few tens and twenties, he noticed.

"Ten dollars you don't eight," said a tall, well-dressed man.

"I'll take that bet," snapped a gray-haired drunk as he shook the dice in his cupped hand. "Come on, eighter from Decatur. Be there, baby," he pleaded, tossing the dice. The two red squares scrambled against the end board of the table and spun to a stop with four white dots showing on one of them and three on the other.

"Son of a bitch! Craps!" muttered the drunk as he stepped back to let Pusser take his place.

When Pusser took his turn, he tumbled the dice around in his hand, studying them closely. Then he threw a seven for six dollars. He let the money ride as he tossed another seven.

Next, he picked up four for a point and made "Little Joe from Kokomo" for twenty-four dollars. He scooped up all the money except a five-spot.

On his fourth roll, Pusser crapped out before making a ten. The dice kept changing hands, and the former Marine kept fattening the wad of greenbacks in his hand.

The next time his turn came around, he flipped out two natural sevens in a row. "That boy's hung up on sevens," someone grumbled.

On his third toss, a house man grabbed the dice, pretending to check them.

Pusser grew tense. "Okay. I saw you switch dice. Let's keep playin' with the other ones," he said.

Suddenly four thugs grabbed Pusser and pulled him away from the table. Two of them pistol-whipped him while their partners smashed him in the face and body with their fists. Pusser tasted blood.

He slumped to the floor, unable to defend himself, then felt a sharp kick in his side. "We'll teach you damned plowboys to come over here and accuse us of cheatin'," one of the hoodlums yelled.

Pusser could feel them going through his pants pockets looking for money. With his dice table winnings, he had about two hundred dollars. When the outlaws were finished searching him, they picked him up, opened the back door, and threw him out onto the gravel driveway. It was still raining.

As he lay sprawled face down in the gravel and rain, half-conscious, Buford Pusser could think only of getting even with them someday. He thought they had gotten away with robbing, beating, and killing people long enough.

Struggling to his knees, Buford Pusser touched his head

with a hand that felt like lead. Pulling a handkerchief from his back pocket, he pressed it against a long gash on the side of his head. Watching the rain mix with his own blood on the ground where he had lain, Pusser felt no fear, only anger. "The sons of bitches will pay for this," he mumbled to himself. "They'll pay for every drop of blood I lost tonight."

He staggered to his Chevy, where he rested a moment, then drove to the Humphrey-Phillips Clinic in Selmer. It took 192 stitches to close the gashes in his head and face.

Buford Pusser had gotten his first real taste of the stateline mob's criminal tactics. Their paths would cross again, and he would get his pound of flesh.

CHAPTER TEN

The hum of circular saws ripping through lumber dominated the cool February air. The noise put a twinkle into the eyes of Jack Hathcock. "Won't be long till we can start nailin' up the framework. Things will go pretty fast then," Hathcock told Pee Wee Walker.

"Yeah. Next thing you know, we'll be right back in business," laughed Walker.

The two state-line mobsters, with the help of five professional carpenters, were busy constructing a new restaurant and motel. They hoped to have it completed by late May 1957.

The restaurant and ballroom would be located where the Forty-Five Grill had sat in Mississippi. The motel would be right next door in Tennessee. Only the imaginary boundary line would separate the two buildings.

Hathcock had decided to name the new establishments the Shamrock Restaurant and Motel. He had borrowed $18,000 from Pee Wee Walker to help finance the projects.

During the construction process, Louise Hathcock separated from Jack. She was careful to keep her whereabouts hidden from her husband, and he spent endless hours trying to track her down.

Because Jack was almost illiterate, he depended solely on Louise to tend to the bookkeeping chores. He loved her shamelessly and had grown extremely close to her during their twenty-year marriage.

Jack satisfied Louise's financial needs. But that did not compensate for his "piss-poor" bedroom performances.

Louise Hathcock was having a clandestine affair with Pee

67

The Shamrock Motel opened its doors for business in June 1957. Authorities said Jack and Louise Hathcock fleeced tourists out of more than $7,000 a week at the Shamrock.

Wee Walker. While Jack combed the state of Mississippi for his wife, his "best friend" was keeping her "sexual garden" watered. Louise and Pee Wee were sliding between the sheets daily at a motel between Corinth and West Point.

Because Pee Wee could no longer use the excuse of having to work every night at the Forty-Five Grill, he was keeping his own wife appeased by spending the late evening hours with her.

Louise's hooky playing was driving Jack insane. He was as rattled as a famished monkey trying to eat an artificial banana. "Where in the hell could Louise be? I've called her mother and all her other kinfolk. Nobody's seen hide nor hair of her. She couldn't have just vanished off the face of the earth," Jack whined to Pee Wee.

"Calm down, Jack. She'll be back. She's just messin' with yore mind. Women's good at that. My wife does it all the time. Just play it cool. Louise will be back," Walker consoled him.

"I hope yore right. I've got to find her. If I find out she's shackin' up with some motherfucker, I'll blow his brains out," Hathcock threatened.

Walker forced a laugh. "Yore lettin' yore imagination run away with you, Jack. I don't think she's fuckin' with nobody. She'll be back. Believe me."

Jack continued his fruitless search for his woman. Suspicious of everyone, he saw culprits behind every tree. He even suspected the sot Howard Carroll. Then he felt ashamed. Carroll, he assured himself, was not attracted to anything he could not drink.

But Pee Wee Walker was another matter. Jack had noticed that Pee Wee hung up his carpenter's apron every day and dropped out of sight for more than three hours. Then he returned and worked a couple of hours more before quitting time.

One evening after Walker had put his carpenter's apron back on, Hathcock confronted him. "Pee Wee, I been wonderin' where you disappear to every day. You always stay gone for three or four hours. You need to be here helpin' me work. The sooner we get this built, the sooner the greenbacks roll in."

The remarks caught Walker off guard, but he managed to keep a straight face. He remained calm. "Everybody needs a breather, Jack. Keeps you fresh as a daisy. Makes you work harder when you get back on the job."

"Bullshit! You don't need three hours to catch yore breath!" snorted Hathcock.

Walker looked into the distance. He saw a hawk circling in the late evening sky. He wished he were as free as the bird, but instead he was shackled by guilt. "I didn't mean to upset you, Jack. I like to visit every day with a bootleggin' friend of mine. We shoot the shit and drink a little booze. He just lives a couple of miles from town."

Hathcock believed Walker's spiel like he believed the moon would plunge to the earth at midnight.

The next morning Pee Wee wasted little time on the job. He quickly went to work helping another carpenter nail together a section of wooden frames.

When the opportunity arose, Hathcock jotted down the odometer reading on Walker's car. After his sidekick left on his daily break and returned, Jack checked the mileage again. He noted that Pee Wee had driven more than one hundred miles. It was less than ten miles—fifteen at the most—to any place on the outskirts of Corinth. He knew that Walker was lying about the visits to the bootlegger.

Before Pee Wee left work for the day, Jack decided to verify his suspicions. "What kind of liquor does your friend peddle?" asked Hathcock.

"Mostly Old Crow. Sometimes he stocks a few half-pints of Jim Beam, too."

"Did you see yore buddy today?"

"Yeah. I go there every day," lied Walker.

Jack Hathcock was convinced that Pee Wee Walker knew Louise's whereabouts. He was also convinced that his "ole friend" was having an affair with her.

After steamrolling into a jealous rage, Hathcock telephoned Walker. "Pee Wee, you been lyin' to me like a fuckin' dog! You know where Louise is at! You been shackin' with her!" Jack fumed.

The accusations did not surprise Walker. He had been expecting Jack to unload on him. He had dreaded it since the day his "friend" first questioned him about his vamoosing routine. "I don't appreciate yore attitude, Jack. I thought we was close friends."

"I did, too! I thought I could trust you! But friends don't fuck their buddy's wife!"

"Hold on now, Jack!"

"No, you hold on, Pee Wee! I'm tired of yore bullshit! I've already spent more than one thousand dollars tryin' to find Louise. You let me spend it when you knew where she was all the time."

Walker was silent.

"Yore a sorry, low-life motherfucker, Walker. Don't you ever set foot on my property again, or I'll blow yore fuckin' head off!" swore Hathcock.

For the first time, anger replaced guilt in Walker. "Don't you threaten me, you chicken-shit sonofabitch! Just pay me the $18,000 you owe me, and then you can kiss my ass," Walker said, slamming down the telephone receiver.

Several days passed. Hathcock and Walker did not cross paths. Then, early one morning, Jack telephoned Pee Wee. "Pee Wee, I been thinkin'. I shouldn't have accused you of messin' with Louise. We been friends too long to let anything come between us."

"You should never have accused me of sleepin' with Louise. That really hurt me, Jack."

"How about meetin' me on Douglas Street about eleven-thirty this mornin'? I'll buy you dinner," suggested Hathcock.

Walker hesitated. "Well, okay. But, Jack, you'd better not try any shit with me."

Jack and Louise Hathcock lived in this house on Proper Street in Corinth, Mississippi, from the late 1940s until they divorced in 1957. The brick structure, trimmed in fieldstone, was elaborately furnished.

"Stop bein' suspicious. I just want us to shake hands, grab a bite to eat, and be ole friends again," Hathcock assured him. But Jack Hathcock had no intention of patching up his differences with Pee Wee Walker.

CHAPTER ELEVEN

Greenflies crawled over the corpse of Everett "Pee Wee" Walker. The insects had already deposited eggs in the nose, eyes, and ears of the carcass. The gangster's body was attired in a red sport coat, dark trousers, a white shirt, and black boots, and it was sprawled face up in a clump of bushes near a gravel road about a mile east of Corinth. A few feet away, a large farm pond shimmered under a bright, late afternoon sun.

James Bragg left his Bell Liquefied Gas Company job at 4:00 P.M. and journeyed to the pond. Shortly after wetting his fishhook, he noticed a red object in the bushes. He tried to ignore it and concentrate on the catfish, but his efforts failed.

Finally, his curiosity conquered him. Jerking his hook from the water, he laid the cane pole on the grassy bank and went to investigate the puzzling red article.

The mystery quickly vanished. Bragg jumped into his pickup truck and sped to a nearby grocery store where he telephoned Sheriff Lyle Taylor. Within minutes, Taylor and Deputy Grady Bingham arrived at the scene.

A .38-caliber bullet had entered Walker's head from behind at the base of his skull. He had also been severely beaten. He had been dead a very few hours.

"It doesn't appear the killers were tryin' very hard to hide Pee Wee's body. Left it out here in the open for God and the whole world to see," Taylor told Bingham.

"Sure looks like they wanted it to be found. Otherwise, they would have dumped it in the pond," replied the deputy.

The sheriff finished questioning James Bragg, then wrote

Former Alcorn County Sheriff Grady Bingham points to the spot where Everett "Pee Wee" Walker's body was found in a field about one mile east of Corinth. Walker, a charter member of the state-line mob, was murdered on June 13, 1957.

in his notebook: "Pee Wee Walker murdered. June 13, 1957. Call received at 4:45 P.M. Body found by James Bragg." Taylor also jotted down the gas company worker's home address and telephone number.

Pee Wee Walker's blue 1956 Pontiac was found parked on Douglas Street in Corinth with the keys in the ignition. Investigators believed the hoodlum had been forced from his car and kidnapped.

Alcorn County Coroner Bill McPeters said that Walker, who was thirty-two years old, died as the "result of foul play by gunshot wound at the hands of an unknown party or parties."

The bullet was removed from Walker's skull, but there was no way to establish which gun had fired it because of its battered condition. Local authorities were convinced that Walker had been murdered by one of his own gang members. Although his demise was not mourned by law enforcement officials, the Walker homicide was given top priority.

Early the next day Jack Hathcock became a prime suspect when investigators learned that the state-line lord had accused Walker of sleeping with his wife. An inside source fueled the flames of suspicion when he told the officers that, during the passionate quarrel, Walker had also demanded repayment of an $18,000 loan.

The investigators believed Jack Hathcock had an unshakable motive: ridding himself of the man who was romping in the sack with his "darling Louise" and erasing an $18,000 debt. District Attorney N. S. Sweat, Sheriff Lyle Taylor, and County Attorney James Hugh Ray all felt confident that Hathcock was "their man."

Jack Hathcock vehemently denied any participation in or knowledge of Walker's murder. He claimed that he had not seen the victim for several days prior to his death and repudiated the charges that he owed Walker money or that the two of them had argued.

Sheriff Taylor, however, uncovered a witness who linked Hathcock to Walker on the day he was slain. A Douglas Street resident said he saw Pee Wee Walker park his Pontiac on the thoroughfare and get into a Cadillac driven by Jack Hathcock at approximately eleven-thirty on the morning of the homicide. At that time, Hathcock owned a red 1955 Cadillac Coupe de Ville with a cream-colored top.

Further investigation turned up several persons who had, on the day in question, seen Hathcock with Bobby Floyd, Dewitt Curtis, and Hershel Roberts. Floyd, Curtis, and Roberts had long been connected with Jack Hathcock and his illegal operations. All were franchised members of the state-line mob.

Floyd, just under five feet, eleven inches and a sharp dresser, was a professional confidence man. The cigar-smoking rogue could have conned a man-hating woman into marrying him. Curtis was stocky and of average height, and his weak eyesight forced him to wear glasses. He was an expert at shuffling cards and tossing dice. Like Bobby Floyd, he smoked cigars. Roberts, tall and thin, was a man of few words. His quiet mannerisms often belied his marble-hard character. All three of the hoodlums were barely in their thirties.

Hathcock and his mobsters displayed their "closeness" to Pee Wee Walker by attending his funeral. Services were held on June 15 at McPeters Chapel; burial was in Henry

Cemetery in Corinth. Survivors included his wife, his mother, and three daughters.

After Walker's burial, rumors circulated that his penis and testicles had been cut from his body and stuffed into his mouth by his slayers. The reports were false. Pee Wee Walker's corpse had not been mutilated in any fashion.

Four days after the funeral, authorities arrested Hathcock, Floyd, Curtis, and Roberts. They were charged with the gangland-style murder of Walker. After all four thugs pleaded not guilty, Peace Justice Buck Sorrell had them jailed in lieu of bonds totaling $25,000. The next day, Hathcock was released on a $10,000 bond. Later, Floyd, Curtis, and Roberts posted $5,000 bail each.

"Those bastards are as guilty as hell. But they keep denying they had anything to do with killing Walker," District Attorney Sweat told Sheriff Taylor.

"They're all ole pros. We'll have to come up with an airtight case against 'em. They won't ever confess to anything," predicted Taylor.

"Hell, no. They wouldn't even confess to being alive," agreed Sweat. "But they're the heart of the state-line rackets. If we could send them up the river, we could put the state line out of business."

The sheriff frowned. "Yeah, but we ain't got no solid evidence against 'em. Got some witnesses who saw them with Walker before the murder, but there ain't no law against talkin' to somebody."

"I'm going to run a bluff on them. I'm going to tell them, if they're not guilty, they'll agree to take a lie detector test," smiled Sweat. The district attorney felt certain that the four gangsters would refuse to undergo a polygraph examination. He was wrong.

Jack Hathcock, Bobby Floyd, and Dewitt Curtis quickly agreed to take the test at the state police headquarters in Jackson, Mississippi. All three of them flunked. Still they stuck to their original stories. They all claimed to know nothing about the circumstances surrounding Pee Wee Walker's demise. Hershel Roberts, believed to have had the least involvement in the murder plot, was not taken to Jackson.

On July 9, 1957, the Alcorn County grand jury refused to indict the four hoodlums. The jurors said there were not enough "solid facts" to warrant true bills for murder. While the authorities were convinced that Jack Hathcock had masterminded Walker's death, the lack of evidence had tied their hands. Nevertheless, Sweat promised, "The case will remain open."

Meanwhile, Jack Hathcock had opened the Shamrock Restaurant and Motel, and Louise had returned to the state line. She promptly informed Jack that she intended to divorce him. He became a basket case.

After listening to Jack whine like a spoiled child for days, Louise finally agreed to stay and help him operate the Shamrock businesses, but only if he would permit her to obtain a "no-strings-attached" divorce. At the time, Jack would have agreed to anything to pacify Louise. The couple reached a pact whereby they would be business partners but completely free of any marital obligations.

On August 28, 1957, Louise filed for divorce in chancery court in Corinth. The divorce was granted on September 10. Under the terms of the decree, "full, complete, and absolute custody" of the couple's adopted daughter was "awarded to Louise without any rights of visitation on the part of Jack." Louise kept the house on Proper Street, and Jack retained the state-line property.

In the meantime, information surfaced that Jack Hathcock had paid a "hit" man named Charles Paul Rothschild one thousand dollars to knock off Pee Wee Walker.

Rothschild, a former Chicago policeman who had soured, was in Corinth on the day of Walker's murder. The ex-cop had been seen with Berry "Junior" Smith, Walter Flanagan, Tex Flanagan, and Herman Childs. The Flanagans operated dives on the outskirts of Corinth, and Childs was a thug who had killed at least four persons.

Rothschild had also been seen with Fannie Bell Barker, who was known as the "Queen of Hearts" from the Phenix City, Alabama, boom days. There she had operated a club by that name. She was an Alcorn County native and now owned the El-Ray Motel south of Corinth.

James Hugh Ray had been appointed county attorney

when his brother H. M. Ray resigned the post and accepted a job in New Orleans. He learned that Rothschild was in jail in Columbia, South Carolina, on burglary charges, and on July 7, 1958, James Hugh Ray telephoned J. P. Strom, chief of the South Carolina Law Enforcement Division. Strom confirmed that Rothschild was in custody there.

Ray agreed to send the chief a detailed letter about the Walker homicide, and he did so immediately. In the correspondence, he outlined every bit of information pertinent to the case so that Rothschild could be thoroughly interrogated.

The letter read, in part, as follows:

. . . For several years . . . Pee Wee had worked for Jack Hathcock, who with his wife, Louise Hathcock, has operated a notorious nightclub . . . at the state line. Their place was formerly known as "45 Grill," which burned. . . . Last spring Hathcock built a new, modern brick building on the same spot known as the Shamrock Restaurant. During construction of the Shamrock, Hathcock's wife, Louise, was away from here, having apparently left Jack, and he reportedly did not know where she was although he tried desperately to locate her. Hathcock . . . had . . . depended on his wife in the management of the business, and in her absence, Pee Wee seemed to have taken over that responsibility.

About the time the Shamrock was completed . . . Jack and Pee Wee had a falling out, and the latter told witnesses he had severed his connections with Hathcock. We recovered letters from Louise to Pee Wee indicating a clandestine relationship between the two, and there were also rumors that Pee Wee had an investment in the Shamrock. Either of those events could have provided a motive for Hathcock to remove Pee Wee. . . . through the years, Hathcock and Walker have had charges of rape (Walker), robbery, and unlawfully selling whiskey filed against them. There have also been . . . mysterious deaths around Hathcock's place which were never solved. There have been no convictions on any of the felony charges primarily because of lack of evidence to indict. . . . Hathcock is one of the most notorious operators in the state, and we believe he brought about the death of Pee Wee but, so far, have been unable to prove that.

Following Walker's murder . . . we filed charges against Jack Hathcock, Bobby Floyd, Dewitt Curtis, and Herschel

Roberts but were unable to secure sufficient proof to get an indictment. Floyd had been and is now employed by Hathcock, and the others have worked for him on occasion. Hathcock, Floyd, and Curtis were given lie detector tests which indicated they were not relating the truth, but none of them admitted any knowledge of the murder. . . .

Our information is that Rothschild has been in Corinth several times and is familiar with and knows Hathcock's crowd and Corinth. At the time in question, Rothschild was staying at the El-Ray Motel about one mile south of Corinth on Highway 45. During that time, he was seen in company with Fannie Bell Barker, known as the "Queen of Hearts" from Phenix City, Alabama, who now lives here and apparently owns the El-Ray Motel, another spot with a reputation for illicit goings on, which is next door to "Theresa's Truck Stop." Other persons whom Rothschild was seen with may have been Junior Smith, Walter Flanagan (operates Rustic Inn), Tex Flanagan (operates Ranch House), Herman Childs, and a companion known only as "Pete" who does not live here.

It appeared that Walker was killed elsewhere than where his body was found, but investigation did not establish where. The places mentioned above are all possibilities with a tourist cabin at the Rustic Inn as perhaps the most likely. Hathcock's car was seen in and around the outskirts of Corinth the afternoon of the murder.

. . . our grand jury convenes next Monday, and we are quite anxious to learn whether Rothschild knows anything about this unsolved murder. . . . Please telephone me . . . as soon as you question him. . . .

Charles Paul Rothschild was questioned extensively by South Carolina authorities about the Walker murder case, but he denied any association with the slaying.

The Everett "Pee Wee" Walker folder was placed in the inactive files in the county attorney's office. It has been gathering dust ever since.

CHAPTER TWELVE

The dark, dreary sky matched Lyle Taylor's mood. It had been spitting snow since noon. The weather threatened to turn really nasty before nightfall.

Taylor entered County Prosecutor H. M. Ray's office. Ray had returned as county attorney after his brother, James Hugh Ray, resigned. It seemed as if the siblings could not decide which one of them wanted the job.

After the customary exchange of greetings, Taylor seated himself in a high-backed wooden chair. The sheriff's fleshy face was distorted with anger. "Damn it to hell! There ought to be some way for us to close down those bastards at the state line. They just keep on robbin', bootleggin', and beatin' the shit out of people. I get complaints every day."

Ray, a short, wiry man in his early thirties, pushed his chair back from his paper-cluttered desk. "Don't you worry, Sheriff. Their days are numbered. We had them hammered to the shithouse wall the last time; then we pulled the nails out. There will be no nail-pulling this time around!"

The two law enforcement officials were still waltzing to the same old tune the Hathcocks had played at the Forty-Five Grill. Only this time, the shakedown ditty was being featured in a brand-new joint called the Shamrock Restaurant, which also had a dance hall.

Taylor and Ray had backed Jack and Louise Hathcock into a corner when they filed court documents to have the Forty-Five Grill padlocked and asked Chancellor William Inzer to permanently ban Jack Hathcock from possessing or selling intoxicating beverages. The county attorney had then set aside the legal papers after Hathcock sold the property and the building later burned. Taylor wished that Ray had not trashed the petitions. If he had continued the court proceedings, Ray could have lawfully barred Jack Hathcock from the whiskey business forever.

Like its predecessor, the Forty-Five Grill, the Shamrock specialized in illegal booze, rigged dice games, card tricks, and young harlots.

Since their divorce Jack and Louise Hathcock had maintained a smooth business relationship at the Shamrock. Both the restaurant and the motel were financial successes. On the personal side of the coin, however, things were more turbulent. Jack resented not being able to share Louise's bed.

At times he insisted that she take a second trip to the altar with him. When he became too pushy, the lioness in her exploded. "We are no longer married, Jack, and never will be again! This is strictly a business deal. Nothing more! If you keep buggin' me, I'll walk outta here, and you can shove the Shamrock up yore ass," fumed Louise.

Her tough stance was effective. Jack would cower like a whipped puppy and beg Louise to forgive him.

Actually, Louise Hathcock had no intention of ever kissing the Shamrock good-bye. She was pocketing piles and piles of greenbacks. Furthermore, she truly enjoyed running the eatery, the dance hall, and the motor inn.

In spite of numerous warnings, the Hathcocks continued to thumb their noses at the authorities.

Late one evening two couples entered the Shamrock dance hall through the rear door. The thrill-seekers had just come from the Rock Pile, a rustic beer joint located on the bank of the Tennessee River near Counce in Hardin County, Tennessee. None of them was feeling any pain as they seated themselves at a middle table.

Frank, a riverboat worker in his early twenties, sat on the far side with his girlfriend. Ralph, a young pulpwood cutter, slipped his left hand under the table and caressed his female companion's crotch. "Watch it. Don't start a fire you can't put out," she laughed. "I need to powder my nose."

Both girls—barely old enough to have pubic hair—sauntered toward the rest room.

Louise Hathcock approached the table. "Howdy, boys. What can I get for you?" she smiled.

"Give us two half-pints of Ancient Age and four Cokes," answered Frank.

"Make that three Cokes. I'm gonna drink mine straight," Ralph interrupted.

"Okay. Be right back." Louise walked away.

Ralph grinned. "I heard that ole gal is tougher than the bark on a hickory tree."

"Yeah. They say she'll smash your head in with a ball peen hammer if you mess with her," Frank whispered to his friend.

The girls returned to the table. So did Louise. "Here you go, boys."

Frank handed Louise a twenty dollar bill. She left as if she were going to get change. More than thirty minutes passed, and Louise still had not brought Frank's money. "I don't believe she's gonna bring me my change," complained Frank. "Whiskey costs $2.50 a half-pint, and Cokes are a quarter apiece. I only owed her $5.75."

"Don't start any shit in here! We don't want to hassle with Louise Hathcock or her goons. A lousy $14.25 is not worth gettin' shot or beat to death over," Ralph cautioned his friend.

Frank lit a Camel. "I know where yore comin' from, Ralph, but it really pisses me off. The money is peanuts. But just think! If they shortchange ever'body who comes in this joint, look at the extra loot they rake in every week."

The couples finished their drinks and left the dance hall. Louise, who was rolling high dice with an elderly man at the bar, watched them go. She laughed to herself.

Frank had not found Louise Hathcock's tactics amusing. He reported the swindle to Sheriff Lyle Taylor. Taylor made another trip to H. M. Ray's office.

The county attorney decided that the petty theft case was too weak to prosecute, so he filed the complaint in his Shamrock folder for future use. "We're moving closer to our goal, Sheriff. Got a lot of violations in the Hathcock file."

Taylor lifted his hat and scratched his bald head. "We'll have more evidence tomorrow. Some undercover folks are gonna gamble and buy liquor at the Shamrock tonight."

"Great. Like I promised you, Sheriff, we're going to cork the criminal jug at the state line."

On March 20, 1958, based partly on the evidence the undercover agents provided, Taylor, Ray, and District Attorney N. S. Sweat, Jr., filed a petition in Alcorn County Chancery Court to restrain Jack and Louise Hathcock from selling whiskey at the Shamrock Restaurant. After reviewing the evidence and listening to various witnesses, Chancellor William Inzer issued an injunction. The decree prohibited the Hathcocks and their agents and employees from unlawfully keeping or selling intoxicating beverages at their state-line roadhouse. County officers warned the Hathcocks that if they violated the court order, they would be arrested and jailed for contempt.

Outside the courtroom the prosecutor reminded the sheriff of Towhead White's pending release from prison. "Got a letter the other day from Parchman. Ole Towhead White is going to be paroled soon. He didn't serve much time on that burglary rap from Quitman County. They just sent him up last year," said Ray.

"Yeah. We need that bastard back here like we need a bucket of shit on the eatin' table," sighed Taylor. "Towhead White is serious trouble!"

Within days after the chancery court hearing, Jack and Louise Hathcock were again peddling booze at the Shamrock Restaurant.

CHAPTER THIRTEEN

The Shamrock Motel sign with its four-leaf clovers bragged about modern conveniences. "Television. Air Conditioning. Pool. Tile Baths. Carpeting."

The up-to-date accommodations impressed Carl Douglas "Towhead" White. He saw them as symbols of financial security that would soon open new doors of opportunity for him.

White, just paroled from Mississippi's prison at Parchman, had now returned to the state line. It was August 23, 1958. Since 1953 he had been drifting in and out of Alcorn County, calling Corinth home.

Towhead White had vowed to become the undisputed boss of the Tennessee–Mississippi border. He had also boasted that he would someday be the Al Capone of the South. The young outlaw was planning to make the Shamrock Motel his headquarters.

White had been sentenced by a Quitman County jury in September 1957 to three years in Parchman. Earlier that year, he had broken into a grocery store in Vance, a small plantation town in the Delta. He planned to burglarize the safe. Instead, he was almost killed.

Crouching behind a counter inside, the store's owner had blasted White through the wide, glass front window with a .12-gauge shotgun. He was rushed to a hospital in Memphis, and four days later he escaped.

The gangster was arrested in June 1957 by U.S. marshals in El Paso, Texas. Charged with unlawful flight to avoid prosecution in Quitman County, he was returned to Mississippi and convicted of attempted burglary.

* * *

Towhead White was born on December 31, 1936, in the Friendship community near Sumner, Mississippi, where his father, W. S. White, was an auto mechanic. His parents separated when Towhead was not yet in grammar school, and his mother, Elizabeth, moved to nearby Clarksdale with his three sisters. Towhead chose to live with his father.

White attended the Sumner Elementary School and was later a star football player with the West Tallahatchie High School Choctaws. He left school early in his sophomore year.

He had his first brush with the law when he was only fourteen. His gambling and fistfights at the 49 E Club, a beer joint on the outskirts of Sumner, inspired several run-ins with the police. Because of his age, the officers merely gave him stiff reprimands and warned him to "straighten up."

Carl Douglas "Towhead" White built a reputation throughout Tallahatchie County for being "as tough as a pine knot." He was as mean as a tarantula. Some said he was the devil incarnate.

White's slender six-foot, 2-inch frame, dark and wavy hair, handsome features, and Dale Carnegie personality worked to his advantage with women and men. He could laugh and joke one minute, and then, with only his soft brown eyes showing the change, turn to solid granite the next. People did just about anything he asked them to do. Those who knew him best said he could have become anything he wanted to be.

What he wanted to be, apparently, was one of the top hoods in the southern part of the United States. Now, at age twenty-one, with Al Capone as his idol, Towhead White was laying the foundation to become the state-line kingpin.

Shortly after his return to the border, he met a dragline operator named Tommy Bivens. White immediately liked him.

Bivens, six-feet, three-inches, 185 pounds, was a part-time member of the state-line gang. He regularly found both pleasure and excitement in the dives when he was not working on his construction job out of town.

He was a modest, calm man until he was angered. Then he became hell on wheels. Almost everyone liked him.

A few days after their first meeting, White asked Bivens if he could bring a couple of young college girls over to Bivens' house. "Man, these chicks are knockouts. Both of 'em are built like movie stars, Tommy. I'll line 'em up for tomorrow night." White's Delta accent had some black pronunciation in it.

Bivens, who was not married, quickly gave his approval. "Sounds like a winner to me," he smiled.

Shortly before 7:00 P.M. the next night, Towhead White knocked on the front door of Bivens' house on Waldron Street in Corinth. "Where's the women?" asked Bivens as he let White in.

"I gave 'em the address. They'll be here pretty soon."

Within thirty minutes, two gorgeous nineteen-year-old girls arrived and quickly made themselves at home. Both were freshmen at Ole Miss in Oxford.

White's date, a friendly blonde named Debbie, could not keep her hands off him. Bivens' gal, a brunette named Marsha, was more reserved.

After the couples downed a few rounds of mixed drinks, Towhead escorted Debbie into the guest bedroom. He did not bother to close the door. Tommy gently pulled Marsha from the couch and led her into his private quarters. He did close his door.

Before Tommy and Marsha could shed their clothing, they heard Debbie screaming, "Damn it, that hurts! Ohh! I'm not used to taking it in the ass! Ohhh. Damn it, Tow! Take it easy! Ohhh!"

Marsha, clad only in her panties, froze. "What is he doing to Debbie? Sounds like he's trying to kill her!"

"He's not gonna do anything she don't want him to do. Everything will be all right. Now let's get in bed and stop worryin' about them," whispered Bivens.

Marsha wriggled out of her underwear.

After their sexual romp, Bivens and his companion lay in bed and chatted for almost an hour. That irritated White.

"What in the hell is the holdup in there, Tommy? You gonna let that broad move in with you?" White, naked from the waist up, was standing outside his friend's bedroom door.

"What's the rush? We'll be out in a minute," snapped Bivens.

When the couple returned to the living room, they found White locked in Debbie's arms. She wanted to spend the entire night with him.

"There ain't no way, Deb. Me and Tommy have got to go back to work at the Shamrock."

"You guys could take us with you. Then, when you get off work, we could all come back here and go to bed," Debbie insisted.

Tommy Bivens liked the idea of a repeat performance with Marsha, but he remained silent.

"Hell, no! We cain't be saddled with a couple of broads while we're workin'. Y'all can stay some other time," promised White.

"You're as stubborn as a jackass, Towhead White. But I love you just the same. You're the only man I ever want. Come on, Marsha. Let's go."

Before the college students could leave the driveway, White burst into laughter. "That stupid bitch! After what I made her do, she still says she loves me."

Bivens thought that White had a cruel sense of humor. He was sadistic when it came to sex. Again, Bivens remained silent.

Towhead White continued to leave lasting impressions on those with whom he came in contact.

One afternoon, White, Jerry McDaniel, and Ron Windsor were in a Corinth pool hall. McDaniel would later be a Corinth police captain; Windsor would become a lawyer, then prosecuting attorney of Alcorn County. The three men, who often hung out together, were waiting for an available pool table.

Suddenly, Dock Carter, another White associate, rushed into the recreation parlor. His face was checkered with black-and-blue spots.

"What in the hell happened to you?" asked White.

"Three goons stomped me over at Neil's Place. They beat me like a stepchild," said Carter.

Ron Windsor was a close friend of Towhead White. He later became a lawyer and prosecuting attorney of Alcorn County, Mississippi.

Anger danced in White's eyes. "Are the sonofabitches still up there?"

"They was awhile ago."

"Come on, everybody. We're goin' to Neil's," ordered White.

The four roustabouts piled into White's Cadillac and headed for the nightspot, which was located near the McNairy–Hardin County line in Tennessee. The large roadhouse was almost as wide open as the state-line joints.

Towhead White slid his car to a stop facing the club's entrance and hopped out. He peered through the spacious plate-glass front. "Do you see 'em in there, Dock?"

Carter nodded. "Yeah. That's them sittin' on the stools at this end of the bar."

White, dressed in an open-necked silk shirt and expensive slacks, turned and walked several steps away from the building. Then, like an Olympic sprinter, he raced toward the entrance. When he crashed through the window, slivers of glass created tiny rivers of blood on his hands and face. He escaped serious injury.

Towhead White could have simply strolled through the

front door. Instead, he chose to impress everyone there by bounding into the club like Superman.

In lightning flurries of fists and dropkicks, White sprawled the trio of roughnecks onto the floor. The fracas was over before it had actually started.

Towhead, who was inordinately athletic, could stand flat-footed and kick the ceiling of a normal-sized room. When he fought, he used a combination of knuckles and feet.

White lumbered back to his Cadillac. Slipping a handkerchief from his back pocket, he wiped traces of blood off his face and hands, then opened the car trunk. He always kept additional clothing in his automobile. His shirt had been torn in the fight, and he quickly changed into a fresh one.

Towhead White ran a comb through his dark, wavy hair, then flashed a wide smile. "Okay, boys. Let's go back to Corinth."

CHAPTER FOURTEEN

Thrill-seekers were swarming the Plantation Club. Loud music and drunken laughter made lipreading a popular method of communication. It was 3:00 A.M., Sunday, December 13, 1959.

Buford Pusser, accompanied by two friends, entered the nightspot, his mind full of memories. He would never forget that night the thugs beat and robbed him, then threw his battered body out into a slow-falling rain. The criminals owed him a debt, and he had come to collect it.

Pusser's friends, who knew why he had journeyed to the dive on this Sabbath morning, were behind him one hundred percent. A shy, patient man, Buford Pusser had waited for two years before deciding that it was time to settle the account.

Pusser, Jerry Wright, and Marvin King, Jr., seated themselves at a table in the dance hall and ordered a round of bootlegged beer. The three men worked together at the Union Bag Company in Chicago, Illinois. All of them were McNairy County natives.

They sipped beer, took an occasional whirl on the dance floor, and waited for the right moment to set their plan in motion.

Pusser did not know the identity of the gangsters who had helped Hathcock pistol-whip him and pilfer his pockets, but he knew that Hathcock had led the attack. Hathcock alone would now have to pay for those sins.

Sometime before 5 A.M., the crowd thinned. Pusser made his move. He approached Hathcock, who was tabulating the cash register receipts. "Howdy," grinned Pusser.

"You'd better hurry up if you want somethin' else to drink," advised Hathcock. "We're fixin' to close."

"Don't need any booze. I need to buy a pistol. Me and my buddies live out of town. Thought we'd feel safer if we had some protection while travelin' back home."

"I got a .32 automatic. Take twenty-five dollars for it."

Hathcock thought he recognized Pusser. But time had blurred his memory.

The club owner exchanged the pistol for money. Pusser briefly inspected the weapon, stuck it into his front pants pocket, and walked away from the bar.

There were still a few stragglers in the joint, and Pusser returned to the table where Wright and King sat nursing a couple of beers. Less than twenty minutes later, the strays cleared out.

Then Larice Hathcock removed her change apron and laid it on the bar. "I'm goin' to bed. It's been a long night," she told her husband.

"Okay. I'll be in pretty soon," he promised.

The couple's living quarters were in the rear of the Plantation Club. The private section had been partitioned off from the dance hall and barroom area. A pressed-wood door led from the honky-tonk into the Hathcocks' apartment. An eight-by-ten-inch sheet of paper with the handwritten word "Private" was thumbtacked to the door.

Except for Pusser and his friends and W. O. Hathcock, Jr., the barroom was empty.

Pusser and Wright strolled to the bar. "Had a good night, didn't you?" Pusser smiled. "Real good crowd."

Hathcock tossed Pusser a suspicious look but ignored the remarks.

When King, who had slipped in behind Hathcock, slammed him over the head with the pistol, the outlaw staggered forward. Pusser battered Hathcock unmercifully in the face, ribs, and chest with a flurry of powerful fists.

W. O. Hathcock, Jr., slumped unconscious to the floor, where Pusser rifled his pockets of one hundred dollars. Then he emptied a cash box behind the bar of $1,176. "Come on, let's go. I got what I come for. Not only did I get my money back, I also got part of Hathcock's ass," he laughed.

When Hathcock regained consciousness, he stumbled back to his living quarters and awakened his wife. She rushed him to Community Hospital in Corinth, where Dr. Frank Davis treated him for deep head lacerations and severe bruises about the body. He confined his patient to the hospital for two weeks.

From his hospital bed, W. O. Hathcock, Jr., signed felony warrants charging Buford Pusser, Jerry Wright, and Marvin King, Jr., with armed robbery and assault with intent to commit murder.

The three men, who had returned to the Windy City, were arrested by Chicago police on January 4, 1960, and held for Alcorn County authorities. They decided not to fight extradition. On January 7, Alcorn County Sheriff Hillie Coleman and his brother, Chief Deputy L. W. Coleman, transported the prisoners from Chicago to Corinth.

Coleman, who had succeeded Lyle Taylor as sheriff, seemed to sympathize with the Hathcocks. He repeatedly taunted Pusser and his two friends with threats of physical harm and vowed personally to see that all of them received long prison sentences. "It's going to be hot as hell down there in those cotton fields at Parchman Prison. And you're all going there. There ain't no doubt about that. Y'all will think I'm an angel compared to them guards. They don't take no shit at all," smirked Coleman.

On January 11, the accused men were taken from their jail cells by Sheriff Coleman and driven three blocks to the courthouse for a preliminary hearing before Peace Justice W. E. Boatman. "You men are charged with taking $1,176 from W. O. Hathcock, Jr., at the Plantation Club on December 13, 1959. You are also charged with attempting to murder him. How do you plead?" asked Boatwright.

All three men pleaded "not guilty."

When the prisoners were unable to post $7,500 bond each, they were returned to jail. With his father's help, Buford Pusser came up with bail money on January 15. King and Wright were also freed a couple of days later.

The Alcorn County grand jury true-billed Pusser, King, and Wright on January 25, 1960. The armed robbery indictment became Case Number 8954, and the assault with intent to commit murder bill was tagged Case Number 8955.

After the indictments Buford Pusser became restless and worried. It had never occurred to him that the grand jury would believe the Hathcock tale.

Carl Pusser, who was Adamsville's police chief, tried to boost his son's spirits. "No use to walk the floor and worry about those sons of bitches over at the state line, Buford. There ain't a jury in the world with a lick of sense that's gonna swallow Hathcock's story."

"Well, I hope you're right, Dad. Maybe the jury will find us innocent."

The Alcorn County Courthouse stood in a clump of trees in downtown Corinth. An early morning sun cut through the branches and danced off the tan bricks of the building, and the sun had bleached the dull gray trim around the windows and roof until it was silvery white. Six gray pillars graced the front entrance. There was no wind, and an American flag hung lifelessly on a pole near the front walk.

Along the walkway old men wrapped in tobacco-stained coats sat on wooden benches, talking occasionally and whittling cedar sticks. "Understand they're pickin' a jury today fer them boys. W. O. Hathcock claims they're the ones that beat and robbed him," one man remarked, wiping tobacco juice from an already brown-splotched gray beard.

"Yep. And I shore don't think that case art to have ever gone to trial," replied another. "They art to turn them fellers loose. That state-line bunch ain't nothin' but out-and-out scum of the earth."

Inside the cavernous upstairs courtroom, Pusser, Wright, and King sat huddled at a long table with their attorney Cary Stovall. Opposite them were District Attorney N. S. Sweat, County Prosecutor H. M. Ray, and W. O. Hathcock, Jr.

After a day-long court session, a jury was finally seated, and early the next morning, the trial got under way. The state elected to try Pusser and his cohorts on the armed robbery charges first.

The jury box was situated on a raised platform on the right side of the judge's bench. Four white, fly-specked lamp globes dangled from the ends of long chains suspended from the high ceiling. The three hundred spectator seats, arranged in a half-circle, were filled. Several onlookers stood.

District Judge Raymond T. Jarvis, a husky man with gray-streaked dark hair, called the Fifth Judicial Court to order. He announced that the state of Mississippi was trying Buford Pusser, Jerry Wright, and Marvin King, Jr., for armed robbery.

Judge Jarvis, who had displayed some sympathy for the accused men, was well aware of the state-line criminals. He detested them. Memories of his dead son influenced his thinking. The young man had been brutally murdered and buried in a woodshed. Although it had never been proven, the jurist felt that state-line thugs had played a role in his son's death. If he were still alive, young Jarvis would have been about the same age as the three defendants.

The state's first witness was W. O. Hathcock, Jr., who testified that the three defendants were "definitely the ones who beat and robbed" him. Then Larice Hathcock told the jury that her battered husband had awakened her in their apartment on the morning of the crime. "He was badly injured, and I drove him to the hospital."

On the witness stand, Dr. Frank Davis verified that he had treated Hathcock on the morning in question and confined him to the hospital for a two-week period. The doctor added that he was not familiar with any details surrounding Hathcock's injuries, nor had he asked about them.

When Judge Jarvis ordered a one-hour lunch recess, few spectators left for fear of losing their seats.

After lunch a string of state witnesses paraded to the stand. Some were regular Plantation Club customers. Others were Hathcock employees. Each one testified that he had seen Pusser, Wright, and King in the club several times prior to the robbery/beating incident.

The first witness for the defense was Buford Pusser. Denying that he was a frequent visitor at the state-line joint, he specifically denied being at the Plantation Club on December 13, 1959. He claimed that he was in Anna, Illinois, on the day Hathcock was bushwhacked and that he had traveled to the small town with his wife, Pauline; his older brother, John Pusser; King; and Wright.

The district attorney attempted to weaken Pusser's alibi. He accused the ex-Marine of skillfully plotting the Plantation trip. "Now, Mr. Pusser. It is plain to see why you carefully planned this trip to the Plantation Club. You had to cover your tracks well. Otherwise, you knew you would be linked to the beating and robbing of W. O. Hathcock because you had every reason to commit this vicious crime. You came back to seek revenge for the beating you received there at the hands of some dice players. Isn't this correct?"

Defense attorney Cary Stovall leaped to his feet. "I object, your honor. The D.A. is bringing in hearsay evidence. There are no official police records to substantiate his charges."

Judge Jarvis sustained the objection.

Sweat knew he was way off base, but he hoped the jurors had been able to catch his drift. He was convinced that Buford Pusser had returned to the Plantation Club to collect an old debt that involved money and pride.

The district attorney failed to punch holes in Pusser's Anna, Illinois, story, however. Pusser's testimony was supported by his wife, his brother, King, Wright, and Wright's mother. The owner of Pusser's rented Chicago apartment verified the time the group left for Anna and the time they arrived back home.

The personnel manager for the Union Bag Company strengthened the defense's case beyond the breaking point. He presented time cards for Pusser, King, and Wright showing that the three men had been at work until 5:00 P.M. on December 12, 1959. His testimony raised the question of whether it would have been possible for the men to drive to Alcorn County by three the following morning.

Sweat argued that the stories told by the defense witnesses were "too pat." "It's as plain as the nose on your face," he smiled at the jury. "The defense witnesses collaborated with the defendants to construct this fictitious tale about a trip to Anna, Illinois."

The case went to the jury at 6:00 P.M., and two hours later the jurors returned with a verdict of "not guilty." Spectators in the crowded courtroom applauded the decision.

Less than a week later, N. S. Sweat and H. M. Ray

dropped the attempted murder charges against Pusser and his friends.

"Other people might let W. O. Hathcock run over them, but he's not going to do it to me," Pusser later told his father. "If he ever fucks with me again, I'll break his neck."

Buford Pusser would tangle with the Hathcocks countless times in the future.

CHAPTER FIFTEEN

Towhead White sat alone in Louise Hathcock's private office in the Shamrock Motel. Several stacks of greenbacks stood on the desk. Within easy reach was his .38-caliber Smith & Wesson.

Howard Carroll was tending the registration desk, and Jack Hathcock was next door in the restaurant. Louise had not yet arrived.

Louise still lived in her house on Proper Street in Corinth with her adopted daughter. She rarely showed up at the Shamrock before 11:00 A.M.

Jack slept at the motel or on a cot in a small room next to the dance hall. Louise strictly enforced her "no-sleeping-together" policy.

White, who was near the bottom of a fifth of Old Charter, fanned through the sheaves of money with his thumb. He had counted $8,673 and decided to tally his "haul" again.

The door handle rattled. White snatched his pistol from the desk.

Louise Hathcock slipped her key into the lock. The safety chain inside prevented the door from opening fully.

"Who's in there?" growled Louise.

"It's me. Don't get your panties in a wad," Towhead laughed as he unlatched the chain.

She threw her arms around him. "Tow! I'm so happy to see you! I haven't slept a wink since you been gone. These robbery trips keep me on pins and needles."

White stepped back from Louise, then reseated himself at the desk.

"Looks like you made a big score. Where did you hit this time?" she asked.

96

The outlaw remained silent as he counted his money again. Louise moved to the desk and stood beside him. "Don't ignore me. It drives me crazy when you try to snub me."

White reached up between her thighs and rubbed her crotch. Even though she was wearing slacks, the intimate gesture excited her. "Come on, Tow! Let's go to bed! Please! I want you real bad."

Towhead White's good looks and ruthless charm had Louise Hathcock's sexual fever running high. She was hopelessly in love with him, but the cunning criminal was not particularly attracted to her. He occasionally climbed between Louise's naked thighs to appease her because he knew that she controlled the Shamrock enterprises. Having her under his thumb was like owning the whole operation.

"Grab that chair, Louise, and I'll tell you about my trip."

Disappointment settled on Louise's face. "Come on, let's go to bed. You can tell me about your trip later."

Ignoring her, Towhead lit a cigarette. "I pulled this job in St. Louis. Me and a cat from New Orleans. We got there just after midnight.

"It was a great big department store. They had a safe as big as this room. I just about had it cracked open when my partner spotted the night watchman comin' our way.

"Damn. We didn't even know they had a night watchman. Our setup man forgot to fill us in on that little detail. I didn't know whether to shit or go blind."

Louise had abandoned her thoughts of sex and was now intrigued by Towhead's safe-burglary drama.

"My partner rushed over behind me. He was shakin' like a dog shittin' peach seeds. I told him to cool it and leave things to me. We crouched behind some boxes.

"When the watchman got close to the safe, he noticed the front had been peeled. He jerked out his pistol. Before he could make a move, I was on him like stink on shit. I beat that sonofabitch senseless. Got blood all over me.

"That safe had over $26,000 in it. Even after we split it three ways, I brought home a nice little pile of loot."

"Why did you split it three ways?" asked Louise.

"Had to give the setup man his share."

Louise again tried to persuade Towhead to take her to

bed. He spurned her passionate advances, claiming that an important business deal had derailed during his two-day trip and he needed to get it back on track as soon as possible. His story was bogus. He simply wanted to get away from Louise.

White sauntered from the motel to the dance hall, where Jack Hathcock, Bobby Floyd, and Dewitt Curtis were fleecing a new batch of tourists.

Towhead, who had been hitting the bottle most of the day, was almost drunk. Alcohol always made him more mean-spirited than usual.

In the dance hall, he spotted a tall, well-dressed stranger, who was watching Dewitt Curtis deal cards in a poker game. White intentionally bumped the man with his shoulder. The stranger attempted to ignore the gangster.

"Hey, you motherfucker! Watch where you're going," grumbled White.

"I'm sorry. I thought you ran into me," the man answered in a polite voice.

"Don't call me a liar, you sonofabitch! I'll beat your brains out!" White screamed as he floored the man with a dropkick. Then he pounced on the stranger and beat him in the face and head with his fists.

The victim's two friends, who had been playing poker, quickly arose from their seats. They picked up their unconscious buddy and carried him outside to their car, then left the Shamrock in a cloud of dust.

"How come you jumped on that guy, Towhead? His pals were droppin' lotsa bread in the card game," complained Curtis.

"Look, Dewitt. You fuck with me, and you'll get a dose of the same thing that sonofabitch got," White threatened the card dealer.

Dewitt Curtis sat back down. He wanted no trouble with Towhead White. Members of the state-line mob had seen him in action many times, and all of them knew that he could back up any threats he made.

The criminal often displayed his pugilistic talents to intimidate the other rogues. He wanted them to know without question that Towhead White was "the cock of the walk."

Several days later, White met an attractive woman in another Alcorn County nightspot. He frequently bar-hopped around the area. Usually, when he picked up a woman at one of the dives, he would bed her, then chase her from his life.

But Joan Rhodes was a different story. She spun Towhead White around in his tracks. After a brief courtship, Joan Rhodes became Mrs. Carl Douglas White on July 11, 1961.

When word of White's wedding reached the Shamrock, Louise Hathcock was stunned. She sedated herself with straight shots of whiskey.

Jack was elated. He believed that with Towhead out of the domestic picture, he could talk Louise into a reconciliation. Hathcock feared White as he would have a man-eating shark. He had never given a second thought to trying to eliminate Towhead as he had Pee Wee Walker.

White never doubted for a moment that Louise Hathcock was furious with him. He knew that she would pay an enormous bounty for his hide at that very moment, and he knew he could have her eating out of his hand again whenever he chose. In the meantime, he planned to avoid the Shamrock.

Towhead White's marriage barely lasted until the wedding bed got warm. On August 26, his wife filed for divorce, charging him with "cruel and inhuman treatment." She claimed that he beat her severely and cursed her and that she "feared for her life."

In the heat of the marital battle, White left on another crime spree. In November 1961 Memphis police arrested him on a parole violation warrant from Mississippi. He had failed to report regularly to his parole officer for the Quitman County burglary sentence.

On December 12 Joan Rhodes White was granted a divorce. Her maiden name was restored.

The Mississippi authorities sent White back to Parchman in January 1962. He had a knack for talking his way out of trouble, and in less than a month he was freed.

When Towhead arrived back in Corinth, he immediately tried to patch up his differences with Joan Rhodes. At first, his ex-wife wanted nothing else to do with him. Then she weakened, and he again sweet-talked his way to success.

The couple remarried on February 1, but the second trip

to the altar turned out to be even more rocky than the first. Joan left White in June, and again she filed for divorce.

Towhead White continued his criminal escapades. He successfully robbed businesses in Iowa and Illinois before being arrested in Kenosha, Wisconsin, and charged with burglary. He beat the rap.

White returned to Corinth, where he tangled with the law again. He was eventually charged with the Christmas Eve 1962 robbery of Rogers Grocery Store in which nine hundred dollars was stolen at gun point. Although the owners, Mr. and Mrs. J. R. Rogers, identified White as the armed bandit who had emptied their cash register, he escaped conviction. The gangster presented witnesses who testified that he was elsewhere when the crime was committed. The Alcorn County grand jury ruled that Towhead White's arrest was a case of "mistaken identity."

CHAPTER SIXTEEN

Berry "Junior" Smith had never drifted far from the criminal nest at the state line. He had worked for the Hathcocks since his arrival there with Towhead White in 1953.

For nine years Smith and White had molded separate outlaw careers. The two hoodlums had remained friends, but they were not as close as they once had been.

Smith—chunky, black-haired, and in his late twenties—had a tricky personality. He could be warm and friendly one minute and cold and vicious the next.

He had adopted Corinth as his home. He was originally from Boyle, Mississippi, a tiny dot on the map in the Delta's Bolivar County.

After coming to Alcorn County, Junior Smith had married Shirley Drewery, a small, feisty woman who had been crippled by polio. Her mother, Emma Drewery, operated a whorehouse on U.S. 45 about a mile south of Corinth. Known as the Nitefall Motel, the establishment was the target of frequent law enforcement raids.

Emma Drewery used the one-story brick building and an adjacent restaurant for gambling, for illegal beer and whiskey sales, and for prostitution. Young girls, both black and white, peddled sex for whatever price they could weasel.

Junior Smith had joined a band of Mississippi burglars in 1960. Still, he found time to maintain his strong ties with the state-line mob.

Early one night Smith was arrested by the Tennessee Highway Patrol near Jackson with a load of booze destined for the state-border dives. He was charged with possessing and transporting bonded liquor valued at $7,500. The troopers found sixty cases of whiskey and vodka, all bearing Missouri tax stamps, in Smith's car and a rented trailer. He later paid a modest fine.

Junior Smith's favorite state-line dive was the Plantation Club. When he was not on the road with other thieves, he dabbled in the rackets operated by W. O. Hathcock, Jr.

On January 16, 1963, Smith was arrested by Alcorn County authorities on a warrant from Hinds County and implicated in one of the largest burglary rings in Mississippi history. Criminal investigators said the ten-man burglary cartel was responsible for $250,000 in thefts in more than sixty robberies. The highway pirates had looted businesses all over the state of Mississippi.

At the time Smith was already on probation after being convicted earlier of receiving stolen merchandise from a bank burglary in Beulah, Mississippi. All the new charges against Junior Smith were later dropped when prosecutors said they did not have enough solid evidence to convict him.

It was not the first time he had wriggled free from the clutches of the law. Smith and two other criminals had been arrested in August 1960 near Hattiesburg, Mississippi, and charged with possessing burglary tools. All three were found guilty, but the state supreme court later reversed Smith's conviction.

After his last brush with the law, Smith spent less time at the state line and more at the Nitefall and El Ray motels. Both establishments were owned by his wife's relatives. The Smiths would later buy the El Ray.

Meanwhile, Junior Smith's old pal, Towhead White, was making plans to return to the Shamrock and Louise Hathcock. His wife had divorced him on March 19, 1963, and he was now footloose and fancy-free. White knew that Louise Hathcock would be "mad as hell" when she first laid eyes on him. He also knew that his honey-coated charm would soon have her on bended knee.

When Towhead arrived, Louise was standing at the front window of the motel office watching Howard Carroll clear the parking area of empty beer cans and other litter.

White surprised her as he bolted back into her life. Then her blood boiled with anger. "Don't come in here, you bastard! I don't want you near me!" Louise shouted as Tow-

head entered the motel office. "You really got balls! Comin'
back here after treatin' me like a pile of shit!"

White forced a smile. "Look, Louise. I know I done you
wrong. Nobody hates it worse than I do. Hell, I made a
terrible mistake. We all make mistakes. Even you. You married Jack. Remember?"

"I don't want to hear your con jobs! Now get out!"

White became as humble and meek as a small, disobedient
child seeking forgiveness from his mother. "I wish I could
leave, Louise. But I cain't. You been on my mind day and
night since I left. It's been pure hell. I learned a lesson I will
never forget. Nobody can ever take your place in my heart."

Louise's resistance melted like a piece of ice in boiling
water, and she rushed into his open arms. "I'm not gonna
lie, Tow. I've missed you somethin' awful. Nobody but me
knows the hurt and misery I've been through since the day
you left."

"It was the biggest mistake I ever made. I don't know
why I married that slimy bitch. It will never happen again if
I live to be a thousand years old. I'll never leave you again,"
White promised.

He stepped back from Louise and lit a cigarette. "Besides, I ain't had time lately for any romps in the sack. I
been busy makin' them almighty dollars. Come on, let's go
to bed. I'm as horny as a sex-starved tomcat."

Towhead White had been busy. At that very moment, he
was wanted by the sheriff's office in Clarke County, Mississippi, for grand larceny. He had been charged with selling thirty-three bogus diamonds for ten thousand dollars.
The actual value of the cut-glass stones was less than
twenty dollars. White had pawned off the phony gems on
Jim Waldrop, the brother-in-law of Lieutenant Governor
Carroll Gartin, and one of Waldrop's friends named Joe
Thornton.

Shortly after White's homecoming, he and Oliver "Nimbo"
Price were behind the Shamrock Motel near the swimming
pool. White, as he often did, was lifting weights.

Price, slender, blond, and just under six feet, was twenty-
six years old. He was a Jack Hathcock protégé, but he idol-
ized Towhead White. Nimbo Price had accompanied White

on a few burglary jobs, and they had also stolen several cars together.

The sound of a car pulling off the highway caught Price's attention, and he stepped through the gateway of a tall redwood fence that secluded the swimming pool area from public view. "Hey, Tow," he called, "come here. There's a nigger parked in front of the motel."

White laid his barbells down beside a wooden bench, then scooped up his pistol from beneath a sports jacket on the ground before hurrying toward his associate. "What's that motherfucker doin' out there?" snorted White. "Don't he know better than to stop in front of this place?"

The black man, paunchy and in his late fifties, was checking a flat tire on the right rear of his battered old Chevrolet.

Wearing a pair of faded Levi's and an "Old Miss" sweat shirt, Towhead approached the stranded motorist. He kept his hand on the revolver in his right pants pocket. "Hey, nigger! Don't you know better than to stop in front of my place?"

"I's sorry, sir. My ole tire went down on me, and I's hadda stop."

"You didn't have to park that pile of junk here. You coulda gone on up the road."

"I's afraid I'd ruin my ole tire."

White jerked the pistol from his pocket. "All you niggers are stupid idiots. If you hadn't stopped here, you'd just have one flat tire on that old jalopy. Now you're gonna have four," White yelled as he shot a hole in the right front tire.

The man, his eyes as large as silver dollars, scrambled into his car and cranked the engine. Before he could drive away, White shot out the other two tires.

White and Price heard the deflated rubber flapping against the pavement as the man drove along U.S. 45 toward Corinth. "I'll bet that sonofabitch don't stop till he gets his black ass home. By that time, he'll be ridin' on the rims," laughed White.

"Yeah. You scared him shitless," Price chuckled.

Towhead White despised most black people. He had very few black friends, and they had been his partners in crime at one time or another. He had even trained his German shepherd, Hitler, to hate blacks. The dog went crazy every time it saw an African-looking person.

Towhead had grown up in a racial hotbed around the small town of Sumner in the Mississippi Delta. He had been taught his entire life that "niggers" were a plague that "white folks" had to tolerate.

He had bitterly resented seeing the national spotlight focused on his hometown in September 1955. He blamed the unwanted publicity on "arrogant niggers."

Hundreds of people had swarmed the Tallahatchie County Courthouse in Sumner when the accused killers of a fourteen-year-old black named Emmett Till were put on trial. Roy Bryant and his half brother J. W. Milan, both Caucasians, had been charged with kidnapping Till from his uncle's shack on August 28, 1955, and murdering him. The youth's body, with a cotton gin fan tied around his neck, was pulled from the Tallahatchie River the next day.

Bryant claimed that Till had wolf-whistled at his attractive twenty-seven-year-old wife during a visit to Bryant's grocery store in nearby Money, Mississippi. During the trial sharecropper Mose Wright pointed a finger at Roy Bryant and J. W. Milan and identified them as the men who had dragged his nephew, Emmett Till, from his shanty.

An all-white criminal court jury found Bryant and Milan innocent of murder. They were not indicted on the kidnapping charge.

On December 3, 1955, another racially inspired trial was held in Sumner. It did not attract national attention.

Elmer Kimbell, a white man and close friend of J. W. Milan, was tried for the shotgun slaying of Clinton Melton, a black service station attendant. Kimbell, a cotton gin owner, had killed Melton after an argument over gasoline. He claimed he had fired in self-defense, but no weapon was found on or near Clinton Melton's body. Once again an all-white jury returned a "not guilty" verdict.

Throughout both trials, Tallahatchie County Sheriff H. C. Strider kept the black spectators in one section of the courtroom and the whites in another. "We've kept the races separated for a long time, and we don't intend to change now," the sheriff vowed.

Towhead White had never before agreed with a law enforcement officer. But he was fully in tune with Sheriff Strider's attitude regarding the races.

CHAPTER SEVENTEEN

Jack Hathcock raced through the Shamrock Restaurant as if he were being chased by the sheriff. He did not stop until he reached a U-Haul trailer parked behind the building. Another load of bootleg whiskey had arrived.

Mack Oaks, who was sitting at a table next to the front door, thought Hathcock was trying to outrun the law again. He was surprised when the sheriff and his deputies failed to show.

Jack and Louise Hathcock had been under a court injunction for several months. The decree prohibited them from selling intoxicating beverages at the Shamrock, but they ignored the authorities.

The Hathcocks had even been arrested and charged with contempt of court for violating the injunction. Although the two outlaws were facing jail terms for defying the court order, they had been able to stall the trial for more than two years. It appeared that the case might be lost indefinitely in the legal—or illegal—quagmire.

Oaks, a young construction worker and part-time farmer, had been waiting for more than an hour for Hathcock's arrival. He had been squirrel hunting earlier that morning, and he planned to swap Jack Hathcock fourteen tree rodents for an equal number of half-quarts of beer.

Another thirty minutes passed before Hathcock returned to the restaurant.

"Where in hell was the fire awhile ago?" asked Oaks.

Jack disregarded the question. He pulled a chair from beneath Oaks's table and seated himself. "How long you been here, Mack?"

"Almost two hours. Brought you some squirrels. They're back in the kitchen."

"Really appreciate it, Mack. Been wantin' some squirrel. Love 'em better than a hog loves slop. I'll trade you beer all day long for squirrels," smiled Hathcock.

He lit a fresh cigar. "Sorry, I didn't see you when I ran through here. I was in a hurry. Had a load of whiskey to stash before Howard Bunch's boys caught me takin' it outta the trailer."

Oaks laughed. "You'd better not let Howard find out you brought your own whiskey in here. He'll have your ass in a sling."

Bunch, a wealthy bootlegger, controlled virtually all the whiskey and beer sales in the Corinth area. He had connections at the courthouse, and those who failed to buy their booze from Howard Bunch did not operate long in Alcorn County.

Bunch also owned the Ranch House, a rowdy joint of ill repute located on U.S. 45 south of Corinth. Bunch and Hathcock claimed to be close friends, but cold, hard cash always seemed to weaken the friendships of outlaws.

"Bunch ain't gonna catch me," said Jack. "It's cheaper for me to pay somebody to haul whiskey from Missouri than it is to buy it from Howard."

The next morning Jack Hathcock arrived at the restaurant earlier than usual. His cook was missing, and he was forced to prepare several breakfasts. More than two hours later, she finally showed up. "Where in the hell have you been? It's almost dinner time," growled Hathcock.

"Had trouble gettin' up this mornin'. I overslept."

"I don't pay you to sleep. You get paid to work here. It's not my job to sweat over that damned grill. I been fryin' eggs and ham for almost three hours now," Hathcock complained.

"Well, I'm sorry. What can I say? I overslept."

"Overslept, hell! Yore just a lazy bitch who wants to lay up on yore ass in bed instead of comin' to work."

With anger flashing in her eyes, the cook smacked Hathcock in the mouth with a closed fist. Then she scratched and clawed him with the fury of a wildcat fighting for survival. "Don't you ever call me a lazy bitch, you sorry, low-life bastard!" she screamed.

Hathcock snatched an empty beer bottle from a nearby shelf and slammed it across the woman's head. Stunned, but still conscious, she ran from the kitchen with blood streaming down her face from a gash in her skull.

Within an hour Jack Hathcock was arrested on an assault-and-battery warrant signed by the cook. The charges were later dismissed when the woman failed to appear in court to testify against him.

A couple of days after the kitchen incident, Bobby Floyd and Dewitt Curtis teased Hathcock about his fracas with the cook. "You mean you couldn't overpower that little ole woman, Jack? You had to bash her in the head with a beer bottle to protect yourself? Hell, she's as skinny as a broomstick," laughed Floyd.

"She might be little, but she's a bundle of pure dynamite," Hathcock frowned.

"I believe I could have held her till she calmed down. It ain't right to hit a woman. Especially with a beer bottle," grinned Curtis.

Jack Hathcock knew that Floyd and Curtis believed he was a coward, and they were rubbing it in. "I know you guys think I'm chicken shit, but I'm payin' you good money to work for me. So that makes me the boss," spat Hathcock.

Then he changed the subject. "I been meanin' to ask you, Bobby. Did you guys have to waste that stupid little shit that raised so much hell last Saturday night about the dice game?"

"No," said Floyd. "We finally got him to see things our way. He went on home."

In an attempt to curb the complaints about criminal wrongdoing at the Shamrock, Jack Hathcock had organized "bird-dog crews" to follow hard losers who had been beaten and thrown out of the roadhouse. If the victims drove past the sheriff's office and out of town, their only trouble was coping with a battered head and the loss of their hard-earned cash. Those who could not be persuaded to forget were usually murdered and their weighted bodies dumped into the nearby Tennessee River.

"I don't want nobody blabbin' to the law. I cain't afford it. Got too much heat now," scowled Jack Hathcock. "Any sonofabitch who even acts like he's not going to cooperate with us will have to end up with a log chain necktie or a pair of concrete shoes."

CHAPTER EIGHTEEN

Trouble lingered in the air like the constant threat of spring storms. It was early May 1964. The state-line veterans had watched the turbulent clouds gathering on the horizon for weeks. Like weather forecasters, they could not predict the exact time the onslaught would arrive, but they knew it was coming.

Jack and Louise Hathcock had been at one another's jugular veins since Towhead White had returned to the Shamrock. Jack was well aware that his ex-wife was hung up on the flamboyant gangster, but he refused to surrender.

Once during this latest round of verbal battles, Louise had again threatened to leave the Shamrock. She had even packed some of her personal belongings. The bluff worked to perfection.

Desperate to keep Louise near him, Jack offered to lease her the motel and restaurant. She jumped on the proposal like a hungry beagle on a helpless rabbit.

On January 1, 1963, Jack Hathcock leased the Shamrock Motel and Restaurant to Louise for a five-year term. She agreed to pay him monthly installments of $583.33; he agreed to make all repairs to the outside of the buildings, pay all utility bills, and keep the property taxes paid.

Jack had built a new nightclub called the White Iris across U.S. 45 and in Tennessee. The dive was located within throwing distance of the Shamrock. Hathcock planned to devote full time to the White Iris, and it would be an ideal spot for keeping an eye on Louise.

Jack Hathcock spent more time at the Shamrock Restaurant and dance hall than he did at his own honky-tonk. Louise did not relish his company, but she tolerated it.

For weeks Jack drank heavily and badgered Louise more than usual about her relationship with White. He increased the pressure on her "to run ole Tow's ass off" from the Shamrock. "Towhead White don't give a damn about you, Louise. He wouldn't piss on yore guts if they were on fire. He's usin' you. Settin' you up like a clay pigeon. Run his ass off before he wipes you out," Jack pleaded.

"You listen to me, you sonofabitch, and you listen real good! I'm tired of you harpin' about Towhead all the time.

"It's yore ass I'm fixin' to run off. This place is legally mine as long as I keep the lease paid. And it's paid up right now for six months in advance. Under our lease agreement the Shamrock is mine for almost four more years," Louise pointed out.

"I care about you. Love you more than anything else in the world," begged Jack. "That's why I leased the place to you. I was tryin' to do the right thing by you."

"Bullshit! You were tryin' to keep me under yore thumb. Thought you could talk me into livin' with you again, but it's over between us. The sooner you realize it, the better off both of us will be."

Hathcock lit a fresh cigar. "Please, Louise, listen to me. I want . . ."

"No! You listen!" she interrupted. "I don't wanna hear another word about Towhead White. You mention him again, and I'll bar you from comin' around here!"

"You cain't bar me. You try it, and you'll damn well be sorry you ever made that mistake," Jack threatened her.

Louise laughed. Loudly. "Oh. You gonna hire a hit man to knock me off like you done Pee Wee Walker? You'd better think twice before you try that shit on me!"

"Yore crazy, Louise. You know I'd never hurt you."

The next morning, Louise told White that Jack had turned up the heat under the pressure cooker. "He keeps buggin' me to run you off. The stress is about to kill me. I threatened to bar him, but it won't do any good. He'll keep right on ridin' my ass."

"That ole thang is crazier than a loony bird," White declared. "He just won't give up. We're gonna have to make a believer outta him."

"We gotta do somethin', Tow. I cain't take much more of his shit."

White slipped a half-pint of Old Charter from his inside coat pocket, unscrewed the cap, and took a drink. "I know how to waste ole Jack without either one of us catchin' any heat," White boasted.

"How you gonna pull that off? If he's found dead, yore the first one they'll suspect. Everybody knows you two hate each other's guts."

"I ain't gonna do it by myself. *We* are gonna do away with Jack Hathcock."

"We?"

White killed the half-pint. Then he lit a cigarette. "Yes. You and me."

Towhead White and Louise Hathcock rehearsed the murder plot repeatedly in the privacy of her Shamrock office. Both learned their roles well.

Louise's private quarters were in Room #1, just around the corner from the registration desk. She slept in the room whenever she decided to spend the night at the motel. A green-quilted spread on her double bed matched the curtains and the carpet. Across from the bed was a polished maple dresser with a mirror, its top cluttered with tubes of lipstick, powder boxes, and hair curlers. An oak desk with a small reading lamp on it sat in a far corner.

On May 22, 1964, Towhead White put the wheels of death into motion. It was 2:00 A.M. "Nimbo Price just told me that Jack is over at the dance hall drunk on his ass. It's time for our deal to go down," White told Louise.

Wearing a light blue negligee, Louise hurried from her office to the registration counter, where Howard Carroll, half drunk and half asleep, was slouched in a green cushioned chair. "Wake up, Howard."

"I ain't asleep, Mrs. Hathcock. Just restin' some." Carroll always called his boss Mrs. Hathcock.

"Go on over to the dance hall and tell Jack I want to see him in my room."

"Sure will, Mrs. Hathcock. Be back in a minute."

Louise rushed back to her private quarters. While she

muffled her screams in a pillow, White beat and bruised her body with his fists. Then he slipped open the cylinder of Louise's five-shot, .38-caliber pistol. It was fully loaded. He clicked it back into place.

A weak knock sounded at the door.

"Do you wanna see me, Louise?" asked Jack.

"Come on in."

Hathcock entered the room and left the door open. He did not see Towhead White lurking in a corner until it was too late.

White emptied the revolver, the bullets crashing into Hathcock's heart, neck, and left side. One shattered the dresser mirror. The fifth slug plowed into a wall near the bed.

Fatally wounded and bleeding profusely, Jack Hathcock managed to stagger from the room. He stumbled almost one hundred feet before falling dead in Alcorn County between the motel and the restaurant.

Because Louise was on good terms with McNairy County Sheriff James Dickey, White had wanted Jack's body to be found in the motel room. He never dreamed that his victim would stagger outside and meet the Grim Reaper in Alcorn County. White and Price quickly moved Hathcock's body to the McNairy County side of the line.

Although Louise Hathcock often kept bootleg whiskey and beer stashed at the Shamrock Motel, Dickey had never attempted to catch her in any wrongdoing there. She maintained a close relationship with him. Towhead teased her about sleeping with the sheriff. She merely laughed.

Louise telephoned Sheriff Dickey and told him that she had killed her ex-husband in self-defense, and Towhead White fled the murder scene before the sheriff arrived. He never liked to chat with the law unless it was absolutely necessary.

Less than thirty minutes later Sheriff James Dickey wheeled into the parking area and climbed from his car. Several persons, including ambulance attendants from McPeters Chapel, were already gathered around Jack Hathcock's corpse. Dickey knelt on one knee and inspected the bullet-riddled body, then released it to the ambulance crew, who took Hathcock's remains to McPeters Funeral Home in Corinth.

"Where's Louise?" asked Dickey.

"She's inside," someone answered.

The sheriff found the motel madam standing alone next to the registration counter. She had slipped into a rose-colored housecoat.

"What happened, Louise?"

"I had to shoot him, Sheriff. He would have beat me to death. Just look at the bruises on me." She extended her arms. Both were splotched with black-and-blue marks.

"He really battered the hell outta you. What started the fight?"

Louise wept, patting her swollen red eyes with a small handkerchief. Severe pain from the beating White had administered was forcing the tears. Louise Hathcock wanted everyone to believe that "having to kill" her ex-husband was more weight than she could shoulder. "I was layin' in bed asleep. Jack came into my room about 2:45 A.M. He woke me up and wanted to have sex. When I refused to let him sleep with me, he went crazy and started beatin' me.

"I jumped outta bed and ran to the dresser and opened the drawer. I grabbed my pistol and started shootin' at him. He turned and left the room. I thought I'd missed him.

"If I hadn't gotten away from him and grabbed the pistol," sobbed Louise, "he would have beat me to death!"

Dickey agreed with her. Without asking to see the murder weapon or attempting to locate any witnesses, he took her to Selmer and called General Sessions Judge Clyde Treece. Louise was released on five thousand dollars bond.

Funeral services for Clyde Raymond "Jack" Hathcock were held on Saturday, May 23, at McPeters Chapel in Corinth. He was buried in Henry Cemetery on the outskirts of town—the same graveyard where the corpse of Everett "Pee Wee" Walker lay rotting under the black Mississippi soil.

Ironically, Peace Justice Buck Sorrell, who had signed the warrant for Jack Hathcock's arrest in the Walker murder case, was one of his pallbearers. Bobby Floyd, who had also been arrested in the Walker case, was another.

During a hearing in general sessions court in Selmer, Louise Hathcock told Judge Treece that she had shot her ex-husband to death because she feared for her life. Sheriff Dickey testified that Louise had been severely beaten and that he believed her claim of self-defense. Judge Treece dismissed the murder charges.

CHAPTER NINETEEN

Jack Hathcock was barely cold in his grave when Towhead White started making plans to line his pockets with Louise's money. He was convinced that she was head over heels in love with him, and he knew that a Cupid-stung woman was the most vulnerable of all earthly creatures. Even though Louise Hathcock worshiped the almighty dollar, White felt sure he could sweet-talk her into the poorhouse.

Towhead had been out of pocket for a few weeks, but he had telephoned Louise and informed her of his whereabouts. He had been arrested by Memphis police on a fugitive warrant and turned over to Clarke County, Mississippi, sheriff's deputies. After days of court bouts, White beat the rap of selling thirty-three bogus diamonds to the lieutenant governor's brother-in-law and another man. Towhead White seemed to have a rabbit's foot for every occasion.

When the gangster returned to the Shamrock, he ordered the cook to prepare specially cut T-bones. That night he drank and dined in the restaurant with Louise. Later he held her on the dance floor and whispered romantic lies in her ears. She believed every word.

The next evening, White and Tommy Bivens were cruising around, drinking booze in Tommy's new Oldsmobile. Bivens had spent most of the day on an out-of-town construction job. Towhead had wasted most of that Thursday with Old Charter.

"Take me back to the Shamrock. I just remembered some important business that needs tendin' to right away," said White.

Bivens was caught by surprise. "We just left there not an hour ago. Thought we were gonna ride around and hit a few joints."

"I need to go back. It won't take long."

Bivens turned the car around near a Corinth city limits sign and headed to the motel. He parked under the canopy. The gravel and tar covered awning was attached to the motel front and supported by two wooden posts. It stretched across a drive-through area.

Bivens followed White inside. Louise was sitting behind the registration counter. "Didn't expect you back so soon, Tow. You either, Tommy," she smiled.

Towhead White got right to the point. "I need some money. Ran into a hot deal awhile ago. It's too good to turn down. I need fifty thousand dollars."

A startled look settled on Louise's face. "That's a lot of money, Tow."

The hoodlum faked anger. "I knew it, you ole thang! You love ole Ben Franklin more than you do me. When it boils down to dollars or me, you cling to the greenbacks!"

"I didn't say I wouldn't give you the money. Yore too hotheaded, Towhead White," Louise snapped as she turned and left the room. Minutes later she returned with a bundle of cash packaged in plastic wrap and laid it on the counter top. "There's the fifty thousand dollars you wanted."

Without saying a word, White scooped up the fifty grand and strolled from the motel office. Bivens was close on his heels.

Traveling on U.S. 45 toward Corinth, Towhead still was not pacified. "That bitch has got more money than this. I want all of her cabbage."

White was almost drunk.

"I think Louise was pretty generous. There's not many damned people who'll give you fifty thousand dollars," Bivens reasoned.

"She should have offered me more. The stingy bitch! Take me back. I'm gonna get every fuckin' dime she owns," boasted White.

"Louise gave you what you asked for. You can get more out of her later. Hell, let's don't go back and hassle her tonight."

"I wanna go back to the motel! If you don't wanna take me, let me out. I'll catch a ride."

Bivens, not wanting to argue, wheeled the Olds around. He wished he had stayed home that night.

Louise Hathcock was still behind the registration desk when White and Bivens again entered the motel. Louise was puzzled. The dust had not yet settled from their last departure.

White slammed the cellophane-wrapped package down on the counter. "Take this money, and shove it up your ass! You didn't bother to see if that was all I needed. You just coughed up what you had to."

"But, Tow, that's all you asked me for. Please don't be upset."

"Don't put them sugarcoated words on me, you selfish bitch! I'm leavin', and I don't ever wanna see your fuckin' face again!"

Louise hurried from behind the counter and locked her arms around the gangster's waist. "Please don't leave me, Towhead! Please listen to me! I love you more than anything, and I mean anything!"

White pulled away from her. "No. I'm leavin' this joint," he bluffed.

"Please don't leave me. You can have every penny I got. I'm beggin' you to stay with me!"

"You really sure that's what you want?" he asked.

"Yes! I've never been more sure of anything in my life. We'll go back to my room pretty soon, and I'll even tell you where I keep my money stashed."

Tommy Bivens already had his hand on the doorknob. He knew that Towhead was going to stay with Louise and put the final touches on his con job.

The old "give in or I'll leave" game had been reversed on Louise Hathcock. Without realizing it she swallowed the very same bait she had frequently tossed to her ex-husband.

CHAPTER TWENTY

Towhead White talked tough, and he was as tough as he talked. Folks wanted no trouble with him. When he called people's hands, they threw in their cards. All except Tommy Bivens.

Bivens, easygoing and soft-spoken, had a "live and let live" attitude, and it took a great deal to ruffle the feathers of the big dragline operator. He had married and later divorced Barbara Drewery. She was the niece of Emma Drewery, who operated the Nitefall Motel and Restaurant. A daughter was born to the union.

White, who had successfully intimidated everyone else at the state line, sensed that Tommy Bivens might not be an easy mark. But talk that he himself was "scared" of Bivens infuriated the gangster. He wanted everybody to fear him.

On June 20, 1964, Towhead White decided to clean the cobwebs from the heads of the "doubting Thomases." That day he vowed to whip Tommy Bivens and crown himself the undisputed champion of the state line.

Only a handful of people were in the Shamrock Restaurant on the "day of reckoning." It was 3:30 A.M., and Tommy Bivens sat alone in a booth. Towhead White and Louise Hathcock sat at a table across from Bivens, arguing with each other. W. O. Hathcock, Jr., and his wife, Larice, had just wrapped up another "day" at the Plantation Club and had settled at a nearby table. Bivens was engaged in idle chatter with W. O. and Larice.

Without warning, White broke off his argument with Louise to turn to Bivens like a venomous snake. "You're a sorry, no-good sonofabitch, Bivens. A chicken-shit mother-

117

fucker. Let's go outside! I'm gonna whup your fuckin' ass," shouted White.

Bivens was caught totally by surprise. He knew the hoodlum was drunk, and he also knew that Towhead White was a dyed-in-the-wool troublemaker when he had spent too much time with old John Barleycorn. Still, Bivens hoped to sidestep a scrape. "What's the matter with you, Towhead? I thought we were friends. I ain't done a thing to you."

"You're lily-livered, Bivens! I'm gonna stomp yore ass and make you like it," snorted White.

"No, you ain't gonna stomp me, Towhead. Nobody's gonna run over me. Especially when I ain't bothered 'em at all," Bivens said in a soft southern drawl.

Towhead scooted his chair back from the table. He remained in his seat. "No use stallin', Bivens. You're gonna get an ass whuppin'. Might as well come on and get it over with."

Bivens realized that he was not going to get out of the restaurant without a skirmish with White, but he planned to let White make the initial move. It came quickly.

The gangster leaped into mid-air and landed on Bivens in the booth. He hammered his stunned "friend" in the face and head with a flurry of fists.

Bivens stood. He jarred White's chin with a vicious right blow, then followed up with several other hard punches to the outlaw's face and chest. Blood splattered.

"Stop it, Tommy! Stop right now!" Louise demanded as she pulled White back from the booth.

"He started this shit. I didn't," snapped Bivens. "I was mindin' my own business, and he jumped on me!"

Both Louise and Towhead ignored Bivens' remarks.

"Come on, Tow. Let's go over to my room," urged Louise. Seconds later the couple disappeared through the front door.

"What in the hell is White's problem?" asked W. O. Hathcock. "Don't understand him jumpin' on you. The sonofabitch is crazy drunk!"

Bivens snatched a paper napkin from a metal holder on the table. He quickly wiped blood from a cut on his lower lip. "I don't know what's wrong with the stupid bastard. I've never done a damned thing to him. He might fuck over

Tommy Bivens was an "old friend" of Towhead White until the gangster tried to kill him at the Shamrock Restaurant on June 20, 1964.

other people and get by with it. But he ain't gonna fuck over me," declared Bivens.

Less than five minutes later, Towhead White stormed through the back door with a .38-caliber pistol in his right hand. "I'm gonna do somethin' bad to your fuckin' ass, Tommy Bivens," he hissed.

"Go ahead. That's what you need is a gun. Hell, you can't fight a lick," Bivens sneered.

Just as White raised the pistol and fired, Bivens turned his head. The bullet struck him in the lower left side of his nose and exited through his right cheek. Bivens threw his hands over the wound.

Towhead White fled the scene.

"Take it easy, Tommy," advised Larice Hathcock. "I'll get a towel to put over your nose to stop the bleeding." After wrapping a kitchen towel partially around Bivens' head, the Hathcocks drove him to the hospital in Corinth.

Shortly after the shooting, White, speeding and crippled by alcohol, slammed his Cadillac into a large poplar tree. The mishap occurred on Boneyard Road, a narrow strip of blacktop that stretched from U.S. 45 to Shiloh Road in Corinth.

A passing motorist picked White up and carried him to the hospital. The gangster told medical personnel that his injuries had been received when his car crashed into a tree. A hospital spokesman, however, told Alcorn County Sheriff

Cleaton Wilbanks that White had been "badly beaten up." The sheriff immediately linked Towhead White's injuries to the Tommy Bivens shooting. He knew that both men wallowed in the same state-line mudhole.

Both Bivens and White refused to give statements to the authorities. Before Bivens was transported by ambulance to Kennedy Veterans Hospital in Memphis, he told Sheriff Wilbanks, "I don't know where I was when I was shot, and I don't know who pulled the trigger."

Late the next evening Towhead White telephoned Tommy Bivens at the Memphis hospital. "Hope you're not pissed at me, Tommy. I'm really sorry about what happened. I want us to stay good friends."

"Fuck you, White! The war is on between us! Don't you forget that!"

"Come on . . ."

A husky female voice paging a doctor over the intercom system temporarily drowned the telephone conversation.

"Come on, Tommy. Don't be that way. You know it wouldn't have happened if we hadn't both been drinkin' that night."

"I hadn't drunk enough to make a piss ant tipsy," snapped Bivens.

"Yeah, but I was drunk on my ass. I even smashed my car into a tree. Don't hardly remember nothing that happened before or after the shooting. I'm gonna come up and visit you."

"Hell, no! I don't wanna see you!" Bivens snorted, slamming down the telephone receiver.

At that very moment, Tommy Bivens hated Towhead White. The outlaw had tried to murder him for no reason whatsoever. Except to pamper his giant ego.

County Attorney Neal Biggers, Jr., and Sheriff Wilbanks visited Bivens in the hospital. Biggers, a pleasant, patient individual, was also persistent. After an hour-long conversation, Bivens finally admitted that Towhead White was the triggerman. The county attorney eventually coaxed a signed statement from Tommy Bivens. It was witnessed by the sheriff.

When Biggers returned to Corinth, he obtained an arrest warrant charging Towhead White with attempted murder.

The moment White learned about the warrant, he turned himself in at the sheriff's office. Peace Justice W. E. Boatman released him on a five thousand dollar bond.

After ten days in the hospital and undergoing plastic surgery to restore his nose, Tommy Bivens returned to Corinth. He "made up" with White, but he promised himself that he would never again trust the "crazy, unpredictable" gangster.

Although Bivens refused to admit it, he was somewhat superstitious. He always carried a buckeye in his pocket. According to an old Indian belief, the buckeye was a good luck charm. Buckeye or not, Tommy Bivens was fortunate to be alive.

At White's preliminary hearing, Bivens retracted the signed statement he had given Neal Biggers and Cleaton Wilbanks in Memphis. "Me and three other guys were fighting in the Shamrock Restaurant that morning. I can't say which one of them shot me," Bivens testified in Peace Justice Boatman's court.

County Attorney Biggers was not surprised. He had known that it would be easier to turn Billy Graham into an atheist than to turn state-line mob members against one another in a court of law. "Without Bivens' statement, we don't have enough evidence to prosecute the case against White," declared Biggers.

The attempted murder charge against Towhead White was dismissed. Although White had used a bullet instead of brute strength to overpower Tommy Bivens, he still considered himself to be the undisputed boss of the state line.

CHAPTER TWENTY-ONE

In the distance, silver clouds churned in a slate-gray sky. A brisk summer breeze spawned whirlwinds, and dampness was cooling the warm July air.

Louise Hathcock hurried into the Shamrock Restaurant and seated herself at a table next to Towhead White. "It's fixin' to rain," she frowned. "If yore car windows are down, you'd better roll 'em up. Might even storm. Looks real bad out there."

"My windows are up. I ain't worried about a rainstorm. I'm worried about that damned shit storm that's brewin' over in McNairy County," said White.

"Shit storm?"

"Yeah. Just heard that big, bad-assed Buford Pusser might be elected sheriff over there. He's still got a hard on for W. O. Hathcock and everybody else at the state line. If Pusser gets elected, the sonofabitch will ride our asses till they're raw," snapped White. "He's a crazy bastard!"

"Pusser *is* crazy," agreed Louise. "He's got an ax to grind with W. O., and he'll ride herd on all of us."

White lit a cigarette. "Got guts, too. Look what he did to W. O. that night at the Plantation. Beat and robbed him like you would a little kid. Pusser's got more balls than a washtub on nut-cuttin' day at a hog farm."

"He's awful young though. Maybe he won't win." Louise sounded hopeful. "People want an older, more experienced man in the sheriff's office. Besides, James Dickey is real popular in McNairy County. Surely the folks over there won't replace Dickey with a young idiot."

"You never can tell," sighed White. "Lotsa strange things happen at the polls on election day.

"Pusser wouldn't get to first base if the people in Mc-Nairy County knew why he was really runnin' for sheriff. He's not tryin' to get the job to help the good, honest folks over there. He wants to be sheriff to satisfy his own selfish pride."

Usually the gangsters paid little attention to the elections on either side of the border. They believed all lawmen had been cut from the same piece of cloth with the same pair of scissors. The sheriffs always arrived on the scene with a Dick Tracy scowl and left with a Beetle Bailey grin.

The hoodlums knew that even honest sheriffs soon tired of bashing their heads against a brick wall. No one man could wipe out corruption by himself. It took a solid chain of law enforcement officials to do that, and the state-line mob had always been able to find several weak links in the chain of command.

The criminals invariably hired slick lawyers and greased the palms of the right people, but Buford Pusser would be an entirely different matter. There would be no loopholes through which to crawl. Pusser believed in fighting fire with fire, and he never buried a grudge.

Louise Hathcock fattened James Dickey's war chest and

Buford Pusser became sheriff of McNairy County on September 1, 1964. At age twenty-six, he was the youngest sheriff in Tennessee history.

secretly campaigned for him at the Shamrock. She did not want to endorse Dickey openly in case Pusser stumbled into the winner's circle. Should that happen, Louise wanted to be able to swear that she had always been in Pusser's corner.

The houses in rural McNairy County were widely scattered. Buford Pusser tried to knock on every door. He solicited votes from sunup to sundown. His campaign promises were always the same: "Elect me sheriff, and I'll put the state-line thugs out of business."

As the election grew closer, Pusser's popularity increased. Promises to rid the state line of wrongdoing always fell on receptive ears among the law-abiding citizens, and the young ex-Marine's voice, with its authentic ring of sincerity, caused people to believe that he would be a man of his word.

Then fate stepped in. On August 1, 1964, two weeks before the showdown at the polls, Sheriff James Dickey died in an automobile crash. The forty-year-old lawman was killed instantly when the 1961 Chevrolet he was driving blew a right front tire, jumped a steep embankment, and slammed head-on into a large tree. The early morning mishap occurred on U.S. 45 a mile north of the state line. Dickey had borrowed the Chevrolet to use while his patrol car was being repaired at a Selmer garage.

Rumors quickly spread that Dickey had been headed back to Selmer after an all-night binge at the Shamrock dance hall. But Sergeant R. L. McClanahan of the Tennessee Highway Patrol said that the sheriff was returning to his office after investigating a traffic accident.

Dickey's body was thrown more than twelve feet from the wreckage. He was pronounced dead on arrival at Community Hospital in Corinth.

In spite of Dickey's death, a large number of voters cast ballots for him, and for a while it was uncertain who would win. When the election sheets were all tallied, Pusser defeated the dead sheriff by a three hundred-vote margin.

Pusser's victory taunted Towhead White and Louise Hathcock. It terrified W. O. Hathcock, Jr.

On September 1, 1964, Buford Hayse Pusser was sworn in as McNairy County's chief law enforcement officer. At age twenty-six he became the youngest sheriff in Tennessee history.

The state-line mob was not concerned with Alcorn County Sheriff Cleaton "Preacher" Wilbanks. He had pinned on the badge early in 1963 after Hillie Coleman fell dead of a heart attack with one year left in office. Coleman's widow filled in for him temporarily until Alcorn countians chose Wilbanks to finish Coleman's unexpired term. Then they reelected Wilbanks to serve four more years beginning January 1, 1964.

Wilbanks, a Baptist minister, was short, paunchy, and in his early forties. He was a neat dresser. Almost everyone called him "Preacher." While he was dedicated to his sheriff's job, Preacher Wilbanks had no clout with Towhead White and the other state-line thugs. They considered him a nuisance rather than a threat.

Towhead White operated the Shamrock and the White Iris Club as if he owned them. Louise had given him a free hand. He had promised to marry her, but he was actually stringing her along so that he could maintain control of the businesses.

Sheriff Buford Pusser often showed up at the Shamrock Motel and the White Iris. Towhead White called it harassment. Pusser called it doing his job.

White decided to "throw a scare" into the new McNairy County sheriff by making some threatening telephone calls to his office in Selmer and his home in Adamsville.

The first call was to Pusser's office. Carl Pusser, the sheriff's father, answered. Buford had named his daddy the jailer and dispatcher shortly after the citizens gave him the sheriff's badge.

"Listen, you old gray-haired bastard, and listen good. There's a ten thousand dollar reward on Buford's head, and I'm gonna collect it."

"Go ahead and collect it, you sonofabitch, if you think yore man enough," Carl Pusser replied angrily, slamming down the telephone receiver.

The second call went to Pusser's house. "We're gonna take your kids out in the swamps and cut off their sweet little heads. That way, the swamp water will get some colorin'," White told Pauline Pusser.

When the sheriff arrived home, he found his wife almost hysterical. Although he was angered by the call, he forced himself to remain calm. He did not want to cause his wife to be any more upset than she already was.

Buford Pusser knew that Towhead White was behind the telephone calls. One of the gangster's so-called friends, who was trying to "butter up" the sheriff, had tipped him.

Late one evening, as Towhead White sauntered from the White Iris Club and crossed U.S. 45 toward the Shamrock Motel, Buford Pusser braked his Dodge between the outlaw and the motor inn. He had been watching the White Iris for more than an hour. "Get up against the car, White, and put your hands on top," Pusser ordered, holding a .41-caliber magnum in his right hand.

"What's the idea, Pusser? You ain't got no right to do this!"

"Shut your damned mouth and do as you're told before you get your head blown off!"

White quickly did a spread-eagle stand against the Dodge. The sheriff searched him and found a .38-caliber pistol in a shoulder holster under his expensive suit coat. "This kind of hardware is illegal. But I'm sure a good law-abidin' citizen like you didn't know that," Pusser snapped as he slipped the weapon into his own jacket pocket.

White made no comment.

Pusser handcuffed the gangster, then ordered him into the front seat of the car.

"You ain't got no right to kidnap me like this," protested Towhead.

"I'm not kidnappin' you. I found a pistol on you, and I'm holdin' you for investigation."

"Investigation of what?"

"Murder, threatenin' telephone calls, robbery. Just name it; you've done it."

"Rat shit! You ain't got a damned thing on me, Pusser, and you know it!"

"Look, White. You called my wife and threatened her with a lotta nasty things. You also called my father. Now you're gonna pay for those calls, you low-life, filthy bastard."

"I didn't make any calls to your family," the hoodlum

Author W. R. Morris examines the handcuffs Sheriff Buford Pusser slapped on Towhead White when the lawman took the gangster to the Hatchie River bottoms and "worked him over."

lied. Always before, he had been able to talk his way out of trouble. But not this time.

Sheriff Pusser turned off U.S. 45 onto Highway 57 toward the Hatchie River.

"Where you takin' me, Pusser?"

"To the river. When I get through with you tonight, you won't be able to make any more telephone calls to anybody."

Fear settled on Towhead White's face. He had always said that Buford Pusser was crazy. Now he was sure of it. "Sheriff! I'm tellin' you the honest truth. I never called your wife or daddy in my life. I swear!"

"I wouldn't believe you on a stack of Bibles. You're a lyin' sonofabitch. You'd say anything to save your own ass. But it's not gonna work with me."

Pusser whipped the Dodge onto a gravel road. The car lights shimmered off the murky waters. A raccoon scampered across the road and into a forest of underbrush. The sounds of bullfrogs echoed through the trees. The entire area was swampy; and when the river overflowed, stagnant water stood for weeks in the bottom lands. On that night, the river was out of its banks.

Pusser stopped the car. "Get out, White!"

"Look, Sheriff. You're a man of the law. You're supposed to protect me, not murder me."

"That's a laugh. A cold-blooded killer like you talkin' about protection of the law. Now get out before I drag you out."

Towhead slid from the seat and stood beside the car. He knew that Pusser was almost insane with anger. For the first time in his criminal career, Towhead White was frightened. "Please, Sheriff, try to understand. I never called your family. Please believe me!" White pleaded.

"Here's the kind of understanding you need," said Pusser as he slammed his fist into the hoodlum's face. White staggered back a couple of steps. The sheriff quickly followed with another punch that caught his victim in the mouth. The state-line thug fell in the soft mud near the edge of the water. Pusser kicked him hard in the jaw. Blood streaked White's face. Buford cocked the magnum. "Crawl, you sonofabitch! Crawl until the elbows and knees are out of that two hundred dollar Italian suit and those fifty dollar Stacy shoes are ruined!"

It was difficult for Towhead White to move with his hands shackled, but he managed.

"I'm gonna kill you, White, then throw you in the river weighted down with iron or chains. You know, the way you and Louise and the other state-line goons do it with all those people you shoot and rob."

White managed to raise himself to his knees. "Please, Sheriff, don't shoot me. I'm beggin' you."

Buford Pusser laughed. He was not going to pull the trigger. That would have been too easy on Towhead White. Instead, he forced the gangster to crawl around in the muddy swamp for several more hours. Then he drove him back to the White Iris.

Careful not to let anyone see his mud-splattered condition, White removed a fresh change of clothing from the trunk of his Cadillac and let himself into a motel room. As he bathed, Towhead White vowed that Buford Pusser would pay for that night.

Later, word circulated about the Hatchie River incident. Many people, including several law enforcement officers, criticized Pusser for taking advantage of a defenseless man who was handcuffed. The sheriff replied, "You have to fight fire with fire."

CHAPTER TWENTY-TWO

The Shamrock was not featured in the Alcorn County tourist brochures. It also missed the "places to visit" list in McNairy County. But the dance hall with its restaurant and motel attracted more out-of-towners than any other place in the area.

In spite of its widespread reputation as a criminal hangout, folks were drawn to the Shamrock like moths to a flame. Even the rumors about the rigged dice games, marked cards, and murders failed to smother the passion for fun and excitement. Countless tourists thought that the impossible odds could be beaten, and when they flunked the test, many complained to the local authorities.

Alcorn County Sheriff Cleaton "Preacher" Wilbanks found himself bogged down in a slough of accusations of racketeering at the state line. County Attorney Neal Biggers, Jr., had also been swamped with reports on the shakedowns at the Shamrock. McNairy County Sheriff Buford Pusser and District Attorney Will T. Abernathy were hearing the same allegations.

Many customers had been lured into the games with free chances on a country ham and from there into a crooked gambling contest with high stakes. Another gimmick was to sell ten-dollar chances on a fraudulent one hundred dollar jackpot. When the losers wanted an opportunity to recover their money, they were forced to put up one hundred dollars against a one thousand dollar pot and so on. Acording to the reports, tourists were being fleeced to the tune of five to seven thousand dollars weekly. An Illinois man said he had recently lost two hundred dollars in a rigged dice game.

Bootleg whiskey and beer were being sold at the restaurant in Mississippi and across the border in Tennessee at the motel and the White Iris. W. O. Hathcock, Jr., had closed the Plantation Club. He did not want to risk another showdown with Buford Pusser.

Liquor sales were illegal in both McNairy and Alcorn counties. Beer had only recently been legalized in McNairy County. No kind of alcoholic beverages were lawful in Alcorn.

Complaints about the "one-way rides" at the Shamrock were nothing new. In March 1958, then County Attorney H. M. Ray and Sheriff Lyle Taylor had obtained a court order prohibiting Jack and Louise Hathcock from possessing or selling alcohol at the restaurant and dance hall. The two officials even cited the Hathcocks for contempt of court after they caught them selling booze in defiance of the decree.

The Hathcocks, who sought out weak links in the chain of justice, had continued to operate their criminal combine. Now Jack Hathcock was dead, and his ex-wife and her lover were still going full blast.

Sheriff Wilbanks was as familiar with the state-line rackets as he was with the Ten Commandments. He knew that it would take more than him and a handful of deputies to throw a monkey wrench into the unlawful operations.

Many citizens, including members of Wilbanks' own Baptist church in Kossuth, were up in arms about the corruption in Alcorn County. The sheriff decided to seek outside help and raid the Shamrock. He planned to arrest all known criminals he found there. Then he would seize the booze and the gambling equipment.

Wilbanks telephoned Governor Paul Johnson at the state capitol in Jackson and asked the chief executive to help him with the Shamrock invasion. The governor agreed to lend his assistance, then turned the cry for help over to Sam Ivy, head of the Mississippi Highway Patrol Identification Bureau.

Ivy, who had in his office a file cabinet full of information on the Hathcocks, Towhead White, and the other state-line hoodlums, was well aware of the criminal wrongdoings at the Shamrock. He promised to be on hand for the raid and to bring fifteen highway patrolmen with him.

Wilbanks also contacted McNairy County Sheriff Buford Pusser and informed him about the planned Shamrock siege. Pusser assured the neighboring sheriff that he could definitely be counted in. The authorities hoped that, with unity, they could buckle the knees of Towhead White and Louise Hathcock.

On Sunday night, December 17, 1964, the lawmen swooped down on the Shamrock Motel and Restaurant like a flock of hawks on a pack of field rats. Passersby mistook the army of uniformed police officers for the National Guard. Reports quickly spread that the state militia had commandeered the Shamrock.

The Mississippi authorities arrested four men in the dance hall and confiscated several pairs of dice. Those taken into custody were Edward Coleman, Bobby Floyd, Clyde Timlake, and W. O. Hathcock, Jr.

On the Tennessee side of the border, Buford Pusser, assisted by his deputies and a host of state troopers, arrested Louise Hathcock. Pusser also confiscated her brand-new Cadillac and a 1962 Ford one-ton truck. Officers found eighteen gallons of moonshine under several burlap sacks in the truck bed and two cases of bonded whiskey in the trunk of Louise's car.

Towhead White was not at the Shamrock when it was raided. He was in Biloxi, Mississippi, making plans to rob the Red Carpet Inn, a notorious gambling joint on the Gulf Coast.

White had hooked up with the Dixie Mafia, a band of traveling gangsters who robbed and murdered people all over the South and Southwest. The Shamrock Motel was his base of operations. It had also become a cooling-off spot for hoodlums hiding from the law.

As one of the Dixie Mafia's top lieutenants, Towhead White often planned murders, robberies, and confidence swindles for the criminal regime. The pack of cunning, ruthless outlaws had been extremely successful at pulling jobs and avoiding convictions.

Louise Hathcock and the others who had been arrested during the attack on the state line were immediately released on bond.

After the raid Sam Ivy told news reporters, "We have

been watching the Shamrock for a long time. It has been confirmed that many ex-convicts from a number of states are using it as a hangout.

"Since Jack Hathcock's death, the Shamrock and the White Iris beer joint in Tennessee have been operated for Mrs. Hathcock by ex-convict Carl Douglas 'Towhead' White."

Coincidentally, Sam Ivy had attended junior high school with Louise Hathcock at West Point, Mississippi. Either she did not recognize Ivy on the night of the raid, or she chose to ignore him.

Two days after the Shamrock invasion, Sheriff Buford Pusser arrested a forty-year-old Selmer man and charged him with possessing illegal whiskey. The man's three-quarter ton truck, loaded with 2,544 half-pints of liquor and 168 fifths, was also seized. Pusser said the whiskey was en route to the Shamrock Motel and Restaurant.

Louise Hathcock's confiscated vehicles had been driven to the state garage in Bethel Springs, Tennessee. Later, they were taken to the auction block in Nashville. On the evening before the sale, Louise gave Hayward King a grocery sack with fourteen thousand dollars cash in it and sent him to the Tennessee state capital to buy back her Cadillac and the Ford truck.

King, lanky, in his mid-thirties with a full head of unruly brown hair, owned a used-car lot in Corinth. He ran with the state-line pack and had been involved in a string of unlawful activities.

In Nashville, King successfully purchased the truck for $4,400, but someone exceeded his bid on the Cadillac. Louise Hathcock wrote the loss off, calling it one of the hazards of her trade. She bought a new Cadillac the next day.

With the stubbornness of Missouri mules, the gangsters refused to bow to the pressures that had been generated by the authorities. They continued to operate as if nothing had ever happened.

CHAPTER
TWENTY-THREE

The state-line corruption pot heated up. While the law battled the blaze relentlessly, the fire seemed to be out of control.

Recently, a college student had been bilked of $135 at the White Iris Club, and two pipeline workers were swindled out of more than $800 in a rigged dice game at the Shamrock.

Towhead White, who had temporarily postponed his heist of the Red Carpet in Biloxi, had returned to his headquarters at the Shamrock Motel. The gangster was furious when Louise Hathcock told him that Buford Pusser had fattened the Tennessee treasury by having her new Cadillac auctioned off in Nashville.

"Pusser's a sorry motherfucker. I knew he would hammer our asses. He's dangerous as a pissed-off rattlesnake," White fumed. "The sonofabitch thinks like a criminal. Look how he beat and robbed W. O., then stomped me while I was handcuffed."

"Yeah, he's a slimy bastard. He didn't have to confiscate my car and truck, but he wanted to fuck with me. We got the truck back, but we had to pay for it twice," frowned Louise.

White removed a pack of Winstons from his shirt pocket and shook one free. "Buford Pusser's a thug himself. He breaks the law whenever he pleases, and nobody messes with him just because he's got a badge. I'm gonna send him a message about the motel raid," White smiled as he lit his cigarette.

Because Pusser had seized the vehicles at the Shamrock and handed them over to the state of Tennessee to sell, Towhead decided to even the score by destroying the sheriff's county-owned car. He carried out his plot on January 14, 1965.

Sheriff Pusser was lured to the state-line area by a bogus telephone call at almost 10:30 P.M. The female caller claimed she had just spotted three men making moonshine whiskey in the woods near her house. "If you hurry right now, you can catch 'em red-handed," the woman urged. She said the illicit still was located in the woods near the intersection of two side roads. The site was about a mile north of the Shamrock.

Towhead White, who had borrowed an old, oil-dripping Chevrolet from a friend, met Pusser on U.S. 45 near the Guys turnoff. The sheriff had his 1965 Dodge floorboarded. White waited for Pusser's taillights to fade in the distance, then wheeled the old Chevy around and headed back toward the state line.

Pusser parked his new patrol car near the "still site." He climbed out and cautiously strolled to a heavily wooded area.

White hid the battered Chevy behind a clump of bushes alongside the road, hastily removed a gallon can of gasoline from the seat beside him, and slithered within sight of Pusser's car. After making sure that the sheriff had disappeared into the woods, the gangster opened the doors of the Dodge and drenched the interior with gasoline. Then he stepped back and tossed a book of flaming matches into the vehicle.

Buford Pusser's patrol car was completely destroyed by the fire.

Towhead raced back to the Shamrock and seated himself next to Billy Garrett at a table in the dance hall. Although he wanted to brag about torching Pusser's car, he decided not to risk telling anyone else about the crime. He had not shared his secret, not even with Louise Hathcock, and he did not intend to.

"Where you been, Towhead? You look a little ruffled," joked Garrett.

"Been lookin' for a good moonshine site," said White.

"The demand for homemade liquor has shot sky-high lately. I can sell all I can make and at a good price."

While the hoodlum had not been scouting for a still site that night, he did plan to launch a full-scale moonshining operation in the near future.

Garrett, who stood just under five feet, eleven inches, was dark-haired and twenty-nine years old. He had a winning personality and a reputation among local law enforcement officials for being "one of the biggest thieves in Alcorn County." His front was a shoe store in downtown Corinth.

"Yeah. You might be on the right track with that moonshinin' idea, Towhead. I hear there's a hot market for it everywhere."

White chain-lit a cigarette. "I'm fixin' to go over to the Stables and see my ole buddy Clyde Garner. You wanna go with me?" he asked Garrett.

"Hell, why not? By the way, where in hell is the Stables?"

"You ain't never been to the Stables? Man, it's a swingin' place. It's over in Henderson County near Lexington, Tennessee."

"I ain't never been there. If I ever was, I was too drunk to remember it," laughed Garrett.

The Stables squatted several yards from a narrow county road in an isolated pocket of Henderson County known as Huron, Tennessee. Because the small community was saturated with Garners, folks had tagged the area Garnertown. The name stuck.

The sprawling nightclub, like the Shamrock, had a far-flung reputation for wide-open gambling, prostitution, and around-the-clock sin. Although it was located in a remote spot, license plates in the parking lot testified that the Stables attracted thrill-seekers from all over the United States.

Several wire-mesh pens full of domestic bobwhites were located off to the left of the parking lot. The most relished fare at the Stables was a southern-fried quail breakfast with homemade biscuits and milk gravy.

Towhead White and Billy Garrett shuffled through the door of the honky-tonk. They were greeted by Clyde Garner, who owned the Stables Club with his wife, Audry.

"Hey, Towhead! Man, I'm glad you come over to see me. Who's your friend?"

"Billy Garrett. He's our kind of people," White confided.

"Great. If you're Towhead's friend, Billy, you're mine. Now if you don't make yourself at home around here, it's your own fault," Garner laughed.

An armed guard in a nearby office eyed the visitors who were talking with the boss. He recognized White from previous social calls. The sentry's job was to keep troublemakers in line and to discourage robbery attempts. The gambling hall, which featured poker, blackjack, dice games, and slot machines, generated scads of money for the owners each night.

Garner nudged White. "You was right, Towhead, about Buford Pusser being a real sonofabitch. He snatched a load of my whiskey over in McNairy County the other day. He wouldn't even talk to me about it. Kept saying for me to tell my story to the judge."

"Yeah, I told you he was a tough bastard to reckon with. He's dangerous. Ain't scared of nothin'. But I'll stop him cold in his tracks one of these days," White promised.

"I hope you do, little man.

"Well, go on back, boys, and enjoy yourselves. Everything is on me. I'll tell my hired hands," smiled Garner.

Clyde Garner, a tall, friendly man in his forties, had known Towhead White for more than six years. They had hauled bootleg whiskey and participated in other illegal activities together. In spite of Garner's outlaw reputation, he was well liked by his neighbors, and his generous contributions to the needy had earned him a warm spot in the hearts of area citizens. Garner would take a man's last dime at the gambling tables, then give him expense money on which to get home.

Back in the dance hall, Towhead White spotted a breathtaking young woman sitting at the bar. He immediately found Garner and inquired about the stunning female.

"She's one of my whores. Usually gets one hundred dollars a throw. If you wanna crack her, it won't cost you nothin'. I'll set it up," said Garner.

"Hell, yes, I want to! She's a knockout!"

The nineteen-year-old hooker escorted White to a

camper trailer behind the nightclub. He spent more than two hours with her.

When White returned to the dance hall, Billy Garrett was dancing with a long-haired blonde teenager. Garner sauntered over to White's table. "Well, how was it?" grinned Garner.

"Best I ever had. I'm thinkin' about takin' her home with me."

"Bullshit. Louise would run you and that whore both off."

The early morning sun was peeking through the pine trees when White and Garrett returned to the Shamrock. Garrett crawled from White's Cadillac, and Towhead drove away before Louise Hathcock could see him.

When White showed up at the motel late that evening, Louise was waiting for him. "Where in hell you been? Shacked up with some tramp? I want some straight answers," she snorted.

"Me and Clyde Garner's workin' on a deal. Was over at the Stables talkin' to him most of the night."

"I don't believe you. I'll bet you spent the night with some young whore!"

"Look, Louise, call Clyde. He'll tell you I was over there. Or you can ask Billy Garrett. He was with me."

Louise calmed down. "Buford Pusser was snoopin' around here this mornin'. Said someone burned his patrol car. He thinks you did it. I told him you couldn't have done it because you were out of town. He seemed to buy the story."

"Hell, I don't know anything about his damned car," lied White. "I was with Clyde Garner. Fuck Buford Pusser."

CHAPTER TWENTY-FOUR

The Alcorn County grand jury sifted through complaints about the criminal wrongdoings at the Shamrock. Past grand juries had done the same thing, but none of them had been able to provide enough lawful muscle to close the dives at the state line.

On January 19, 1965, the new grand jury decided to pay a surprise visit to the Shamrock. The jury members hoped to catch the racketeers off guard and confiscate ironclad evidence against them on the spot.

District Attorney Jack Doty, armed with a search warrant, escorted the grand jury to the notorious restaurant and dance hall. Louise Hathcock could have easily been mistaken for the "Welcome Wagon" hostess. She invited everyone inside and offered them coffee and Cokes on the house.

Louise was expecting her "special guests." A telephone call had warned her that the district attorney and his party were en route to the Shamrock.

A diligent search of the premises turned up no contraband. One member of the grand jury said the place was as "clean as a hound's tooth."

The district attorney was convinced that Louise Hathcock had been tipped off. He also believed the "rat" was holed up in the courthouse. "Louise Hathcock had been warned that we were coming. She quickly got her house in order. There is no doubt that the telephone tip to Mrs. Hathcock came from the courthouse," Doty told news reporters.

The Shamrock shakedowns continued. That same night,

Hayward King parked his Harley-Davidson in front of the restaurant and hopped off. He shied away from the trouble that was in full swing between the eatery and the motel.

Louise Hathcock, Bobby Floyd, and Nimbo Price were watching another thug named Pete Tice shatter the windows in a Buick with a twelve-gauge shotgun.

"Please don't wreck my car! Please! It's all I got to drive to work. I've already lost more than a hundred dollars in your place tonight," a pudgy, middle-aged man begged.

"Shut yore damned mouth. We'll teach you to trot yore ass up here and accuse us of cheatin' you outta yore money," growled Louise.

"I'm sorry! I didn't mean to accuse you of stealin' my money. I'm sorry. Please don't batter my car up any more."

Everyone ignored the man's pleas. Louise spotted King and walked to where he stood. She had her back to the car-wrecking scene.

Tice, who had already broken out all the windows in the Buick, decided to warp the hood with the gun barrel. The weapon discharged.

"Ohhh! Ohhh! I've been shot in the ass!" Louise screamed. She danced in circles, clasping her buttocks with her hands.

"Calm down, Louise. Yore gonna be all right. It's nothin' serious," King consoled her.

"Damn! My ass is on fire! It's stingin' like hell," Louise whined.

"Don't worry. Yore gonna be fine. Come on. I'll take you to the hospital," said King.

He opened the door on the passenger side of Louise's Cadillac. She knelt on the front seat with her rear toward the dashboard. "It's killin' me, Hayward. Ohhh!"

"Just take it easy, Louise. We'll be at the hospital in a few minutes."

King drove Louise to Community Hospital in Corinth. An emergency room doctor said she was not seriously injured. He removed the buckshot from her buttocks, gave her some medicine for pain, and sent her home.

"That scared me, Hayward," Louise frowned on the way back to the Shamrock. "When you get shot, the first thing that crosses yore mind is death."

"Hell. It'll take more than a little buckshot to do you in, Louise. Yore tough as whit leather."

"Hayward, I want you to promise me somethin'. Promise me right now."

"You know I will if I can. What is it?"

"When I die, I want to be cremated. Then I want you to climb on top of the Shamrock Motel and scatter my ashes all over the state line."

"What about yore family? They'll be in charge of stuff like that."

"I'll write it in my will. I'll put in there that I want you to dispose of my ashes after I'm cremated."

"I promise you then that I'll do exactly what you told me to," King assured her.

Immediately after arriving at the Shamrock, Louise Hathcock went to her private room. Towhead White had been gone for two days, but this time she knew where he was.

White was back in Biloxi, Mississippi, finalizing plans to stick up a Gulf Coast gambling casino. On March 25, 1965, the crime went down.

In the early morning hours, three masked bandits armed with tommy guns entered the Red Carpet Inn on the West Beach resort strip in Biloxi. They forced the manager to hand over $11,500 in cash, then lined several customers against the wall and rifled their pockets.

At the time of the robbery, Towhead White was gambling in the casino. He was the only person in the club who was not "roughed up" by the thieves, and when that bit of information was passed on to the police by the casino manager, White was arrested. He was still gambling in the Red Carpet several hours after the holdup, and he was taken into custody at a blackjack table.

White was charged with being an accessory to armed robbery, locked up in the Harrison County Jail at Gulfport, and held in lieu of ten thousand dollars bond. He denied any connection with the Red Carpet heist, but the authorities insisted he was the ringleader of the submachine-gun-wielding hoods who had stormed the gambling hall.

"Carl Douglas 'Towhead' White organized and skillfully

plotted the robbery of the Red Carpet Inn. He engineered it from start to finish," Chief Criminal Investigator Herbert McDonnel told the news media.

Louise Hathcock, through a professional bail bondsman, posted Towhead White's ten thousand dollar bond. The gangster was not in a talkative mood when he returned to the Shamrock.

"What went wrong in Biloxi, Tow?" Louise asked.

"I don't wanna discuss it."

Without saying another word, White left the motel and drove to his rented house in Corinth. He slept until almost noon the next day, then telephoned Pearl at Billy Garrett's downtown shoe store. He arranged to pick her up when she finished work.

Just after dark the next evening, Sheriff Buford Pusser and James Harvell cruised past the White Iris Club. Harvell, who would later become a lieutenant with the Selmer Police Department, was an avid admirer of Pusser. Occasionally, the sheriff would invite Harvell to ride with him.

Pusser slowed his unmarked car. "Looks like ole Tow and the gang have been sellin' a lotta beer. There's a slew of empty boxes piled up behind the joint," Pusser frowned.

"From the looks of things, business is really boomin'." Harvell agreed. "The fools just keep flockin' in to get robbed and shot."

"Yeah. It's hard to nail White and the Hathcocks. They're all shifty bastards. They break the law every day, but it's hard as hell to catch 'em in the act," the sheriff complained.

Pusser turned the car around and headed back toward the White Iris. Parking near the back of the club, he removed a book of matches from the dashboard, then climbed out.

After he quickly scanned the area, Pusser lit the matches and tossed the entire book into the pile of boxes.

As he drove away, he kept his eyes glued to the rear view mirror. A smile creased his face when he saw flames slowly devouring the cardboard crates. "Maybe the damned joint will burn down. Be a blessin' to everyone if it does."

Except for the charring of several concrete blocks and the loss of seven cases of whiskey stashed beneath the boxes, little damage was done to the White Iris.

CHAPTER TWENTY-FIVE

A bright morning sun sifted through the budding treetops and formed peculiar shadows on the whiskey still below. True to its tradition, March was leaving like a lamb.

Towhead White had organized a three-state moonshine network, and business was booming. He was having problems keeping the production ahead of the demand, and his five-man crew worked full time. Those on the payroll were Jack Newton, Bobby Gene Vandiver, Ray Troxell, Donald Dawson, and Tommy Bivens. Construction jobs had slowed to a crawl during the winter months, and Bivens decided to take up the slack by working in the woods with White.

"That mash about ready to run?" White asked Newton, who was huddled over a rust-pitted barrel.

"Looks ready to me."

White poked his index finger into the mash, then licked it. "Man, that's gonna make some mouth-waterin' whiskey. Put it in the cooker."

The moonshiners had a 1,500-gallon distillery. The cooker was fueled by a propane gas burner, and water came from a nearby creek. The illicit operation was hidden in a clump of woods in McNairy County less than two miles from the state line.

Once the mash was in the cooker, the still began to percolate like a giant coffeepot. Dawson placed a five-gallon lard can under the copper spigot, and within minutes, slush belched from the spout, followed by a stream of clear, raw liquor. The whiskey was dumped into fifty-five-gallon metal drums and then siphoned into glass gallon jugs with a garden hose.

Towhead White lifted a jug, turned it up to his mouth, and took a couple of good swallows. "Whew! That's some fine whiskey. It's way better than the store-bought. Smooth as Jack Daniel's," he boasted. "Get it on the pickups. This load goes to our contact in Alabama.

"I've got a business appointment. Got to go. Catch y'all later," White smiled.

Towhead White was raking in more than six thousand dollars weekly from his whiskey racket. He was selling the untaxed liquor in Tennessee, Mississippi, and Alabama.

The next morning at the Shamrock Restaurant, White had breakfast with Nimbo Price. Both hoodlums were eating eggs and country-cured ham. "You still makin' whiskey in McNairy County, Towhead?"

"Yeah. Shipped out a load yesterday evenin' about sundown."

Price asked the waitress to refill his coffee cup, then offered White some advice. "You'd better get your ass outta McNairy County. That damned Buford Pusser is on a rampage. He's already hit a bunch of stills and busted a slew of moonshiners."

"I know it. I don't feel safe there. Pusser hates me anyway. Of course, there ain't no love lost. But I'm fixin' to move my operation to Tishomingo County, Mississippi. Already got a spot picked out there."

"Sounds like a good move. Any place is better than McNairy County."

The two men finished their meals, and White lit a cigarette. "Yeah. I'll be moved outta there in a few days."

Price ordered a fresh cup of coffee and leaned back in his chair. "A friend of mine told me that Paul Moore has been moonshinin' in McNairy County for a coon's age. Wonder why Pusser hasn't busted him?" Price asked.

"Hell, Moore and Pusser are tight. Like twins joined at the hip. The bad-ass sheriff don't bother his close friends."

"I'm not takin' up for Pusser, but everybody does that. A man ain't worth his salt if he won't look out for his ole bosom buddies."

"Well, I say more power to ole Paul. If he can run whiskey without Pusser gettin' on his ass, he should do it. He seems like a pretty nice guy. I've met him a few times over at his beer joint," said White.

Paul Moore, a small, wiry, even-tempered man in his late thirties, owned and operated Moore's Place, a honky-tonk located on Highway 57 near Michie, Tennessee. He had long dabbled in the illegal whiskey business. At the time, Moore was operating a fifty-gallon still near the Gravel Hill community.

Sometimes thieves from the state line dipped into Moore's whiskey stock. Only recently, Leroy King had used a car that belonged to his cousin Hayward King to haul off seventy-four gallons of moonshine from Paul Moore's barn. Moore had spotted King leaving his farm, but when confronted, Leroy King denied taking the booze.

On April 2, 1965, Towhead White moved his whiskey operation from Tennessee to Tishomingo County, Mississippi. The still site was located two miles north of the Crossroads community near Pickwick Lake.

Before White and his roustabouts could open shop, the authorities raided them. On April 6 Tishomingo County Sheriff James Bishop and three federal revenue agents pounced on the illegal brewmasters. Acting on a tip, the lawmen had been hovering around the still site for three days.

Tommy Bivens, Ray Troxell, Jack Newton, Bobby Gene Vandiver, and Donald Dawson were taken into custody on the spot. Towhead White managed to avoid being captured there, but he was later arrested in Corinth. All the moonshiners, including White, were released on bonds of one thousand dollars each.

Towhead White sorted through his mental notes. He could not think of a single person who might have ratted on him to the law. Finally, he consoled himself with the theory that some stranger probably saw him hauling the whiskey rig to the site and snitched him off.

It had taken the county and federal wrecking crews less than thirty minutes to wipe him out. He lost more than twenty thousand dollars in equipment and supplies alone, not to mention the income from the unlawful liquor sales.

The gangster was in a nasty mood when he left the White

Paul Moore operated a far-flung moonshining business in McNairy County during Buford Pusser's days as sheriff. Moore and Pusser were close friends. Members of the state-line mob often dipped into Moore's illegal whiskey stock.

Iris Club. He had already been in a heated lovers' quarrel with Louise Hathcock. Unable to drown his troubles in alcohol, he was in a reckless frame of mind.

White crawled into his Cadillac and drove to the Ranch House on U.S. 45 South. After downing some more whiskey, he started to leave but was stopped by a friend who talked him into leaving his car parked at the roadside dive.

White summoned a taxicab. He wanted to go to the Phillips Brothers' Truck Stop on U.S. 72 West. The restaurant there had a Class A rating for food. "Keep the meter runnin'. Won't take me long to eat. Be right back," White told the cabdriver.

An employee, peering through a large plate-glass window from inside, saw White stagger from the taxi. He knew that the outlaw was drunk and that he was a real hell-raiser when he was in that condition.

The truck stop worker, who was holding a long lug wrench in his right hand, met White at the door. "We don't want no drunks in here, White. Take your damned business someplace else," the man said, holding the glass door partially open.

"You're a stupid sonofabitch if you think you can keep me outta there," White snorted as he attempted to force his way inside.

The employee quickly slammed the gangster in the head

several times with the tire tool. White stumbled backward from the door, blood streaking his face.

Scrambling into the cab, he ordered the driver to take him back to the Ranch House. There he got into his Cadillac and headed toward the state line. Less than a half-mile from the Shamrock, he crashed head-on into a pickup truck.

Towhead White was taken by ambulance to Community Hospital in Corinth, where he was treated for the injuries from the traffic mishap and from the tire tool bashing. Doctors kept him in the hospital overnight and released him the next day.

Less than a week after his brief hospital confinement in May, White left for a crime spree in Texas, Louisiana, and Arkansas. He linked up with an ex-convict named William Mansker Clubb, who was also a member of the Dixie Mafia. Clubb was a known burglar, forger, and hit man.

Before Towhead White returned to Alcorn County in August 1965, he had made the list of the "Ten Most Wanted" criminals in Texas. Authorities said White and Clubb had committed a string of crimes together in the Lone Star State. White squeaked by, clear of all the charges.

In the meantime White had been indicted by a Harrison County, Mississippi, grand jury on charges stemming from the holdup of the Red Carpet in Biloxi. He remained free on ten thousand dollars bond.

On September 15, 1965, Towhead White and his crew of moonshiners appeared in federal court in Aberdeen, Mississippi, and pleaded guilty to manufacturing and selling untaxed whiskey. Sentencing was delayed until September 24.

On that date the White liquor gang again journeyed to the federal courthouse in Aberdeen. Corinth Police Chief Art Murphy appeared on White's behalf and asked the judge to show leniency. Many people wondered why Murphy, who claimed to be one of the state's most dedicated law enforcement officers, would lend a helping hand to a ruthless gangster like Towhead White.

U.S. District Judge Claude Clayton sentenced White and Jack Newton to three years each in prison. Bobby Gene Vandiver received a two-year prison term, and Donald Dawson was handed an eighteen-month sentence in the federal penitentiary. Tommy Bivens and Ray Troxell were placed on eighteen months' probation.

Towhead White was immediately transported by U.S. marshals to the federal prison camp at Maxwell Air Force Base in Montgomery, Alabama. On October 16 he was taken to court in Biloxi to face evidence linking him to the Red Carpet heist. He pleaded guilty to being an accessory to armed robbery and received a two-year sentence to run concurrently with his federal liquor term.

Officials would learn over the next couple of months that not even prison could bridle Towhead White's criminal escapades.

Back at the state line, violence continued. On November 1 a pistol duel at the White Iris left sixty-year-old Woodrow Nixon of Corinth dead. Sheriff Buford Pusser arrested Robert Brewer, also of Corinth, and charged him with Nixon's murder.

According to witnesses, both men had been drinking heavily when they started arguing outside the club. Nixon fired four times at Brewer with a .22-caliber pistol. All four shots missed their mark. Brewer hastily sought cover behind the building, then stepped back out and fired twice at Nixon with a .38-caliber pistol. One bullet slammed into Nixon's chest, and the other one struck the left side of his face.

The charges against Robert Brewer were later dropped when General Sessions Judge Clyde Treece in Selmer ruled the man had fired in self-defense.

A few days after the shoot-out at the White Iris, Pusser was talking with Sheriff Wilbanks in the parking lot of the Shamrock Restaurant.

"Reckon this state-line corruption will ever end, Buford? They just keep on murderin', stealin', and pullin' con jobs here," frowned Wilbanks. "I preach about all this sin almost every Sunday in my church."

"We gotta stay on 'em, Preacher. Things oughtta slow down some with Towhead White in the pen. Keep your chin up. We'll lick 'em one way or the other. In the meantime," smiled Pusser, "just look at the material you're gettin' for your sermons."

CHAPTER TWENTY-SIX

The white Plymouth streaked down U.S. 45 toward the Shamrock Motel, the red speedometer needle hovering near the 100-mile-per-hour mark. Sheriff Buford Pusser was on his way to arrest Louise Hathcock.

Chief Deputy Jim Moffett shifted restlessly on the seat beside Pusser. Deputy Peatie Plunk fumbled with his wide-brimmed hat in the back seat.

Pusser whipped the car off the highway into the parking area of the Shamrock and climbed out with Moffett and Plunk at his heels. It was 10:15 A.M., February 1, 1966. Pusser had two warrants in his pocket—one for theft, the other for illegal possession of whiskey—both to be served on Louise Hathcock.

A young couple, Mr. and Mrs. George Vogel from Benson, Illinois, hurried toward Pusser and the deputies. The Vogels had been standing in the shadows of the motel. "We're the ones who called you about the robbery. I'm George Vogel."

The sheriff was surprised to find the complainants at the motel. He had expected them to drive up after he arrived. "I'm Buford Pusser, the sheriff here in McNairy County."

The man glanced toward the motel office, which was less than a hundred feet away. "My wife and me were robbed of $125 by Mrs. Hathcock.

"We've been here a couple of days. Then, about an hour ago, we decided to go back to Illinois, so I went to the office to pay our tab."

His wife interrupted. "Honey, you'd better not tell them. Let's forget the whole thing and go home. You know what that woman said."

148

"I'm not worried now that the sheriff and his men are here," said Vogel.

"That's right, ma'am. Don't worry about that woman in the motel there. She's not gonna hurt you," Pusser promised.

"Well, when I went to pay our bill, Mrs. Hathcock noticed the amount of money I had in my wallet, so she told me to empty it on the counter top. At first, I thought she was kidding. Then I realized she wasn't when two big goons walked up beside her."

Again he glanced toward the office. "She told me that I wouldn't get hurt if I'd just quietly put my wife in the car and drive back to Illinois. She warned me that if I called the law, my wife and I would both end up in the Tennessee River."

"Louise Hathcock wasn't kiddin'. She's mean as a barrel of rattlesnakes," Pusser said. "A lot of other people she robbed *did* wind up in the river."

The woman shuddered and moved closer to her husband. "I told you, honey. We should have left when she told us to. I'm scared to death!"

"Now, you heard what the sheriff here said. He'll handle things, so don't worry. Everything is going to be all right."

Pusser asked the young man to sign the theft warrant. Then he and the deputies entered the motel office.

Louise Hathcock was sitting at a small desk behind the registration counter examining a set of receipt books. She was wearing a white duster and a pair of red house shoes. A glass nearly full of bourbon and Coke rested on the edge of the desk. She looked up, surprise frozen on her face. She had not seen the sheriff and his deputies arrive.

"Got a warrant for your arrest, Louise. You've been charged with robbing a man and his wife of $125."

"Who signed the warrant?"

Pusser had asked the couple to wait in his car while he served the arrest document. "An Illinois man. Said you robbed him."

"That's a crock of shit! I ain't clipped a soul outta anything. Where's the sonofabitch at? He won't tell me that to my face!"

Louise Hathcock's face was flushed. She had been in the

whiskey bottle all night, and she had also been on the telephone until daylight arguing with Raymond Lee Jones, the husband of her adopted daughter. The feud had ignited when Jones told Louise she could no longer visit with her granddaughter. Jones, who was not particularly fond of Louise, had been very blunt about his decision. Before slamming down the telephone receiver the last time, Louise had sworn to kill Raymond Lee Jones.

"I'm not gonna argue with you, Louise," Pusser said firmly. "You've been charged with robbery, and you're under arrest. You're goin' to jail, and that's that!"

Pusser moved back from the counter. "Keep an eye on her, boys, while I look around for some booze."

In a few minutes he returned, carrying a half-case of Yellowstone whiskey. "I'm also chargin' you with illegal possession of liquor."

Louise stood. "Now listen, Pusser. I can explain this whole situation. Let's go to my private office where we can talk without interruption."

"We can talk right here."

"No. I got some things to tell you. I'm gonna level with you about the whole operation. I wanna talk to you alone."

"Okay. But make it snappy."

"Let me get my drink. I need somethin' to calm my nerves," Louise said, walking to the desk and picking up the glass with her left hand.

Pusser ordered Louise out of the office first, then followed close behind to her private room. It was within those same four walls that her ex-husband, Jack Hathcock, had met his doom.

When Louise unlocked the door, Pusser was surprised at the neatness of the room. Hangers of cleaned clothes in cellophane bags hung on the inside doorknob.

Louise pushed the door to shut it, but the clothes swung between the lock and the catch. The door crept open. Slowly, she slid her right hand into her duster pocket and withdrew a .38-caliber pistol, the same revolver Towhead White had used to murder Jack Hathcock. Still holding the mixed drink in her left hand, she pointed the pistol at Buford Pusser. "You sonofabitch! You ain't takin' me nowhere!"

Pusser jumped back, bumping the edge of the door as

Cathy Morris displays the actual whiskey glass Louise Hathcock was holding when Sheriff Buford Pusser shot her to death on February 1, 1966, at the Shamrock Motel.

Louise fired. The impact from the collision with the door sprawled him across the bed. The bullet plowed plaster from the wall.

Louise Hathcock dropped the glass of whiskey to the green-carpeted floor and ran to the bed. Aiming the pistol directly at Pusser's head, she squeezed the trigger again. The click of the hammer striking the shell in the chamber sounded like a stick of dynamite exploding in his ears.

Buford Pusser scrambled to his knees on the bed, unholstered his .41-caliber magnum, and fired. The bullet caught Louise in the left shoulder and spun her around. The second shot struck under her right arm, tearing a large hole through her heart and lungs. Mortally wounded, she raised her pistol again. Pusser's third shot plowed through Louise's left jaw. Blood and particles of teeth spurted onto the green curtains. Louise Hathcock clutched her chest with both hands, then slumped to the floor with a slowness that fascinated Pusser. He could not take his eyes away. For a moment he watched the blood spew from the wounds; then he holstered his magnum.

Hearing the shots, Moffett and Plunk rushed into the room. The deputies were almost shocked to find the sheriff still breathing. They had been sure that Louise Hathcock had led Buford Pusser into a trap and murdered him. "You all right, Buford?" they asked in unison.

"Fine. But I wouldn't have been if her gun hadn't mis-

fired. Don't move her or touch anything until the T.B.I.
[Tennessee Bureau of Investigation] checks the place," said
Pusser as he left the room.

Pusser slid into a chair in the registration office. He was
numb with how close he had come to dying.

Howard Carroll came into the office and slouched down
in a chair. His unshaven face was white, and he trembled
uncontrollably. "Mrs. Hath . . . Hathcock is . . . is dead,
ain't she?"

Pusser did not answer.

Carroll's faded blue eyes fell on the whiskey case.
"Please . . . please, Sheriff. I nee . . . need a drink real . . .
real bad!"

Pusser did not argue the point. He dug a half-pint from
the cardboard case and handed it to Howard Carroll. Hands
shaking, the old drunk held the bottle to his lips and drained
the contents in one steady swallow.

After the T.B.I. agents had combed the shooting scene,
Louise Hathcock's body was taken to the hospital in Selmer and then to Shackelford Funeral Home. Medical tests
revealed that she had .248 percent alcohol in her blood,
much more than enough for her to be considered legally
intoxicated.

Louise's corpse was later transferred to McPeters Funeral Home in Corinth. Bill McPeters, owner of the mortuary, immediately contacted Towhead White at the federal
penitentiary in Alabama and informed him of Louise
Hathcock's death.

White told prison officials that Louise was his fiancée
and business partner, and his request for a funeral furlough
was approved. While the gangster had made many empty
promises of marriage to Louise, he had never intended to
exchange wedding vows with her. His sole business interest
at the Shamrock now was the large cache of greenbacks he
knew Louise had kept hidden there.

On February 2, Towhead White, accompanied by a U.S.
marshal, arrived in Corinth. The two men first went to the
funeral home and viewed the corpse of Louise Hathcock,
then journeyed to the Shamrock Motel.

White, the only person who knew where Louise had
stashed her money, uncovered the loot hidden in a wall be-

hind the utility room. The cash, totaling $150,000, was in 50- and 100-dollar bills stuffed inside large-mouthed cold cream jars.

White asked his federal custodian to drive him to a wooded area near the state line where he buried the money. He had enclosed it in a waterproof steel box. The marshal, who was not with White in Louise's private office when he counted his haul, did not know how much money the hoodlum had. Because White and Louise were business partners, the federal man thought the cash belonged to Towhead White. Later, Louise Hathcock's heirs would complain that someone had stolen her money, but no fingers were ever pointed directly at White.

After visiting the funeral home again that evening, Towhead hosted a shindig fit for royalty. He ordered thick T-bone steaks, tasty side dishes, and numerous cases of beer and whiskey. Several members of the state-line gang were on hand for the event.

White also arranged for a couple of attractive teenage whores to spend the night with him and the marshal at the Shamrock. The federal officer thought Towhead White was a real southern gentleman.

This small stone marks the grave of Louise Hathcock in the Greenwood Cemetery in West Point, Mississippi.

Louise Hathcock's funeral was held early the next morning, February 3, in McPeters Chapel. After the services her body was transported to West Point, Mississippi, where she was buried with simple graveside ceremonies in Greenwood Cemetery. The criminal career of the South's modern-day Bonnie Parker had finally ended.

Meanwhile, back in McNairy County, after checking the T.B.I. reports of the Louise Hathcock shooting, District Attorney Will T. Abernathy felt that Buford Pusser had killed the state-line madam in self-defense. The D.A., however, presented the case to the grand jury for official action. The jurors wasted little time in ruling that Louise Hathcock's killing was justifiable homicide, and the case was closed.

On December 11 Towhead White and another inmate named Julius Oliver French walked away from the minimum-security prison camp at Maxwell Air Force Base in Montgomery, Alabama. French, twenty-eight, was from Decatur, Georgia. He was serving a four-year term for interstate transportation of stolen property.

White still had some unfinished business at the state line. He wanted to dig up Louise Hathcock's money that he had stashed under the watchful eye of the U.S. marshal and hide it elsewhere.

While quietly tending to his own personal matters, White suddenly found himself chin-deep in troubled waters again. Late on January 2, 1967, McNairy County Sheriff Buford Pusser was shot by an assailant on U.S. 45 about three miles from the Tennessee–Mississippi border. Towhead White became the prime suspect.

Pusser claimed he was shot by the driver of a late model Chrysler containing two males and bearing a Mississippi license plate. The sheriff said he was unable to identify his attackers.

Pusser was struck by three .25-caliber bullets. One slug entered his left cheek and exited cleanly through his right jowl. A second shot burned a superficial flesh wound on h left arm, and the third one grazed his abdomen.

Federal, state, and local authorities launched an intensive manhunt for Towhead White. The officials, misled by false information, were barking up the wrong tree.

Buford Pusser had been shot by Pearl, his black girlfriend. The lovers' quarrel exploded into violence when Pusser accused Pearl of having a secret rendezvous with White and demanded she reveal the gangster's whereabouts.

In an interview with a Memphis news reporter, Pusser said, "I do not think Carl Douglas 'Towhead' White either drove or occupied the car from which I was gunned down. I do think White was closely connected with the shooting."

Pusser knew that Towhead White was not the triggerman and that White's only connection with the assault was the outlaw's close relationship with Pearl. White was totally innocent of any direct involvement in the shooting of Pusser.

Two days later Towhead White surrendered to prison authorities in Montgomery, Alabama. French remained at large. White refused to say where he had been or what he had done while he was a fugitive.

CHAPTER
TWENTY-SEVEN

Towhead White had memorized the game plan. The chess pieces were all in place. If White's king could avoid being captured, Buford Pusser's name would soon be chiseled in stone.

From his prison cell White had sealed a "kiss of death" contract on Pusser with Dixie Mafia king Kirksey McCord Nix, Jr. Nix, the son of an Oklahoma appellate court judge, was one of the most dangerous criminals in the southwestern part of the United States. Nix and White played in the same league.

The Oklahoma-born gangster had handpicked three other professionals for the Buford Pusser murder team: Carmine Raymond Gagliardi, a Boston thug with mob ties in the East, and Dixie Mafia hit men George Allen McGann and Gary Elbert McDaniel.

Nix had already been to McNairy County. Using Towhead White's blueprints for the ambush, Nix had made several practice runs.

Now, on this Saturday morning—August 12, 1967—the would-be assassins spun the wheels of death into motion. The ringing telephone rousted Buford Pusser from sleep. It was 4:30 A.M.

"Hello," he answered drowsily.

"This Sheriff Pusser?" the caller inquired.

"Yessir."

"There's serious trouble brewin' on New Hope Road.

Three or four drunks are threatenin' to shoot it out with each other. There's gonna be a killin' if you don't hurry on down here! If they're gone when you get here, they said somethin' about goin' on up to Hollis Jourdan's beer joint."

"I'm on my way."

Pusser quickly slid into his tan sheriff's uniform while his wife Pauline slipped into a pair of dark brown slacks, a white blouse, and black loafers. "I'm going with you, Buford. I'm already wide awake. And your mother is watching the kids," said Pauline.

The Pussers were looking forward to a family reunion with Pauline's relatives on Sunday. They were already packed and planning to leave for Haysi, Virginia, early the next day.

With the two of them in the front seat, the late-model Plymouth sped out of Adamsville at ninety-five miles an hour, heading west on U.S. 64.

"Wonder what the trouble is all about?" Pauline asked as she shoved a cartridge into a stereo tape player under the dash.

"I don't know. Probably a bunch of drunks tryin' to kill each other."

The sounds of country music vibrated softly from a rear speaker.

"Hope it isn't anything serious," sighed Pauline.

Pusser turned off U.S. 64 onto the blacktopped Gilchrist Road, which twisted its way through gently rolling hills to Stantonville. There he made a dogleg turn across Highway 142 onto Peeble Hill Road, which stretched six miles to Highway 57.

"You got everything ready for us to leave tomorrow?" he asked.

"All but a few odds and ends. Are we going to leave early?"

"Thought we'd try to be on the road by seven. If that's all right with you."

At the stop sign, Pusser slowed, then turned right onto Highway 57. It was only five more miles to New Hope Road. The rough, narrow strip of pavement was approximately seven miles long.

Pusser touched the brakes, and Pauline grabbed a door

handle as the Plymouth whipped onto New Hope Road. The sheriff glanced at the automatic shotgun next to his right knee. Out of instinct, he felt for the holstered .41-magnum pistol on his side.

Farmers were already in the barns feeding and milking cows. In the east, redness was creeping into a cloudless sky, and the woods along the road were alive with morning sounds. "This is going to be a beautiful day," Pauline observed. "Makes you want to live forever."

Up ahead, behind the red-bricked New Hope Methodist Church, Kirksey Nix and his band of killers waited in a sleek, black Cadillac. They had a clear view of New Hope Road.

Within seconds, the hired assassins would earn their blood money. The tombstones in the nearby church cemetery were grim harbingers of death to come.

Pusser kept his eyes on the road ahead, where he expected to see trouble at any moment. In their concentration, neither he nor Pauline saw or heard the black Cadillac approaching from behind.

"We ought to be gettin' close to the spot where the trouble's supposed to be," said the sheriff, turning the steering wheel to dodge a large hole in the road.

The slayers of Pauline Pusser were hiding behind this country church on the New Hope Road waiting for Sheriff Pusser's car to pass. They quickly pursued and ambushed the Plymouth in which the Pussers were riding.

Pauline Pusser was killed during the early morning hours of August 12, 1967, as she rode with her husband on rural New Hope Road in McNairy County. Sheriff Buford Pusser was seriously hurt in the ambush.

Suddenly, the Pussers heard the roar of an engine, and the long, black car was beside them. Orange flames belched from a .30-caliber carbine. The window on the left side shattered, spraying Pusser's face with slivers of glass. The shots missed him and slammed into Pauline's head.

She moaned, grabbing her husband's arm as she slumped down in the seat. Pusser floorboarded the Plymouth. His only thought was escape. He had to get help for Pauline.

Buford Pusser knew that he did not have a chance against the assassins in the semi-darkness with his wife dying beside him. The two guns he had in the trunk were useless to him, and he had not even had time to use the automatic shotgun or the magnum he had in the front with him.

Pauline—he had to get help for Pauline.

Pusser drove two miles down the road and skidded to a stop, thinking that he had escaped the killers. Gently, he placed Pauline's head on his lap. When he saw the gaping hole in her head, he was sick with fright and rage. "Oh, God, please don't let her die! Please, God, don't let her die!" he prayed aloud.

Then the black Cadillac appeared again. This time, a vol-

McNairy County Officials inspect the 1967 Plymouth in which Pauline Pusser was murdered and Sheriff Pusser was critically injured. The car was riddled with eleven high-powered rifle bullets.

ley of shots riddled the car at point-blank range. Pusser caught two slugs in the lower jaw, and his whole chin dropped to his chest, held only by a flap of skin. He sank to the floorboard as another bullet ripped through the metal door and shattered Pauline's skull. Blood soaked the seat, the floorboard, and the occupants.

The ambushers fled, thinking Buford Pusser and his wife were both dead. When the sheriff was sure that the assassins were not coming back, he gripped the steering wheel and pulled himself up in the seat. He looked at Pauline and knew at once that her life had been snuffed out. The bastards, he thought, had failed in their efforts to destroy him physically, but they had succeeded in destroying the most vital part of his life by killing Pauline.

Although Buford Pusser was critically wounded, he placed his hand on his wife's warm cheek and promised to avenge her murder. "I love you, Pauline. Only God knows how much I love you. They'll pay for what they done to you. This I promise," he mumbled.

Pusser was taken to the medical facility in Selmer, then transferred to Baptist Hospital in Memphis. Shelby County sheriff's deputies, fearing the assassins might return to finish their job, stood guard outside the door of his hospital room around the clock.

State, county, and federal law enforcement officers swarmed the ambush scenes on New Hope Road. Authorities found fourteen empty .30-caliber cartridge cases. The bullets used in the attack all contained soft-nosed lead slugs. Chief Deputy Sheriff Jim Moffett and T.B.I. agent Warren Jones found eleven bullet holes in Pusser's Plymouth.

The investigators concluded that the ambush was motivated by Buford Pusser's campaign to clean up the illegal activities on the state line. The shooting of Louise Hathcock and the threats made by Towhead White were mentioned.

The authorities launched a full-scale search for the murderers, and Paul Johnson, governor of Mississippi, ordered his state's highway patrol to aid in the investigation since the ambush had occurred close to the state line.

Kirksey McCord Nix, Jr., was named by Buford Pusser as one of his wife's assassins. Nix is currently serving a life sentence in a Louisiana prison for murdering a New Orleans grocer.

At the request of District Attorney General Will T. Abernathy, Tennessee Governor Buford Ellington offered a five thousand dollar reward for information leading to the arrest and conviction of the slayers. Bill Smith, owner of the Walgreen's drug store in Selmer, raised an additional $2,500. No one ever collected the $7,500 reward money.

Eighteen days after the slaying, Buford Pusser came home. While he was in the hospital, Pauline had been laid to rest in the Adamsville Cemetery.

Although a Memphis plastic surgeon had worked long and hard on Pusser, cutting, stitching, and wiring bones and teeth, his face remained scarred and broken. The doctor said it had been struck by at least two high-powered bullets and possibly three.

Buford Pusser was sure that Towhead White had masterminded the murder, even though it was impossible for him to have been the actual triggerman. He was convinced that White had arranged the "contract" for the slaying.

Again, he vowed to himself that Towhead White and the others who were responsible for his wife's death would someday pay for their crime.

CHAPTER
TWENTY-EIGHT

Violent deaths, like biblical curses, seemed to plague the Hathcock family. Early graves had become as real to the Hathcocks as life itself.

On December 4, 1967, Jack and Louise Hathcock's nineteen-year-old adopted daughter was murdered by her husband, who then killed himself.

Raymond Lee Jones, with whom Louise had argued the last night of her life, executed his wife, Jeanette Susan, with a single shot from a .32-caliber derringer. Then the twenty-four-year-old Jones took his own life with the same weapon. Both victims died from bullet wounds to the head.

The murder and suicide occurred in the couple's Corinth home. Their three-year-old daughter, Karen Jeanette Jones, was in the house at the time of the shootings, as was Barbara Anderson, Susan's cousin.

Miss Anderson told authorities that Raymond and Susan were arguing during a late lunch. They abruptly left the kitchen and went into their bedroom. A few minutes later she heard two gunshots.

Jones, who was employed at Darr's Midtown Gulf in Corinth, had been distraught for more than a month.

Deputy Sheriff Creekmore Wright said that the gunshot victims were in opposite corners of the bedroom when he arrived at the scene. Mrs. Jones was dead, and her husband was unconscious. He died three hours later at Magnolia Hospital in Corinth.

George Coleman, Alcorn County coroner, said that testimony at the inquest revealed that the couple had been having marital problems for several weeks. Jones had also exhibited suicidal tendencies and had threatened to kill his wife.

Death erased the troubles of Raymond Lee and Jeanette Susan Jones. But their departures created new problems for their survivors. The kinfolk of Louise Hathcock wanted Susan buried beside her adopted mother in the Greenwood Cemetery in West Point, Mississippi. The Jones family wanted her laid to rest next to her husband in the Oak Grove Cemetery in Chewalla, Tennessee.

Personnel at the Coleman Funeral Home in Corinth were preparing both bodies for burial. George Coleman, the coroner, owned the mortuary.

After much bickering and an onslaught of hostile words, it was finally decided that Jeanette Susan would be buried in West Point and her husband interred in Chewalla.

Mancel Jones and his wife were awarded legal custody of their granddaughter, Karen Jeanette. The child became confused when her grandparents began to drive her to West Point to visit her mother's grave and asked why her parents were not together.

Jones, who had never been happy with the segregated burials, obtained legal authorization to have his daughter-in-law's body exhumed and reburied next to his son in the Oak Grove Cemetery. The Hathcocks disapproved, but they did not fight to halt the disinterment.

At last, a feud involving a Hathcock had been settled without a single shot being fired.

CHAPTER TWENTY-NINE

Gangland guns had failed to exterminate Buford Pusser. But, like the first cannon's roar at Fort Sumter, the shots on New Hope Road launched a civil war. This time, instead of skirmishes between the Yankees and the Rebels, the battle would be fought solely by a gritty sheriff and a ruthless outlaw.

Towhead White bristled with anger each time he thought about Pusser's "stroke of pure luck." The big lawman was supposed to be dead. White marveled at the fact that Pusser was still breathing. He kept asking himself how the sheriff had survived the barrage of high-powered rifle slugs that ripped away half of his face and left his wife a corpse beside him.

White was not bent out of shape over the bungled murder attempt. He realized that victims marked for assassination were sometimes like Daniel in the lions' den. A supernatural power seemed to snatch them from the jaws of death.

Now, with his prison release just days away, White was planning to return to the state-line area and finish the job left uncompleted on that August morning in 1967. The gangster knew that he was Buford Pusser's prime suspect in the New Hope Road ambush. His outside contacts assured him that Pusser believed White had masterminded and bankrolled the lethal shooting.

Towhead White thought that patience and caution were the key ingredients needed to cook Buford Pusser's goose. Common sense told him that a man who had suffered a nearly fatal snakebite would not stroll barefoot through tall grass.

During his one-year lockup at the Federal Correctional Institution in Texarkana, Texas, White had been a model prisoner. His Sunday school behavior earned him an early parole from his three-year whiskey sentence.

Carl Douglas "Towhead" White arrived back in Corinth on Sunday morning, September 22, 1968. He immediately contacted his old friend Police Chief Art Murphy. The chief and local undertaker Bill McPeters had visited White and had corresponded with him while he was in prison.

After an exchange of greetings, White asked Murphy to telephone Alcorn County Sheriff Grady Bingham. White, who had clashed with Bingham when Bingham was a deputy under Lyle Taylor, wanted to make a stab at smoothing things over with the new sheriff. The gangster knew that the lawman thought more of a shithouse rat than he did of Towhead, but White had always enjoyed a challenge when the odds were not in his favor.

Art Murphy and Grady Bingham were not friends. Their relationship was strictly limited to law enforcement. Murphy had been Bingham's staunchest rival in the sheriff's race. Bingham crushed Murphy at the polls by 1,707 votes and took office on January 1, 1968.

Bingham, fifty-five, slender, dark-haired, and slightly short-tempered, took pride in his job. He was the first Alcorn County sheriff to have standard deputy uniforms and specially painted patrol cars.

The sheriff was preparing to leave with his family for church when the telephone rang. "Hello."

"Sheriff, this is Murphy. How you doin' this mornin'?"

"Fine."

"I got a fellow in my office who wants to talk to you. Could you come down here?"

"I'm fixin' to go to church. Cain't it hold?"

Murphy hesitated. "It's ole Tow. He really wanted to talk to you."

Bingham was not surprised that Towhead White was in Art Murphy's office. The sheriff knew that White and Murphy were bosom buddies, and he believed that White had donated a large wad of greenbacks to Murphy's unsuccessful bid for the sheriff's post. "I ain't got time to come down there. Like I said, I'm gettin' ready to leave for church. I'll talk to him on the phone. Put him on."

Murphy quickly handed the telephone receiver to White. "Hey, Sheriff. How you makin' it?"

"All right."

"Sheriff, I just wanted you to know that I've gone straight. I'm gonna walk clean from now on. I've learned my lesson."

"I'm glad to hear that, Towhead. It always makes me happy to hear that a criminal has reformed. Glad you're makin' plans to travel a straight road."

Bingham did not believe a word of White's spiel. "If you're really goin' straight, I'm behind you one hundred percent. But I wanna give you some good advice, Towhead. Don't try to run over the people I represent cause it ain't gonna work. I'll be on you around the clock. You know that I know you, and I know what you stand for. So you'd better not pull any more of your rackets in Alcorn County."

White lit a cigarette. "You don't have to worry about me, Sheriff. I'm a changed man. Besides, I'm not gonna be around here much. I'm gonna be spendin' most of my time in north Alabama."

"Well, don't forget, Towhead. When you're in my county, you'd better walk the straight and narrow," Bingham declared.

Shortly after his conversation with Bingham, White telephoned McNairy County Sheriff Buford Pusser. "Hey, you motherfucker! You're livin' on borrowed time. You're a dead sonofabitch!" White smirked, slamming down the receiver.

Pusser recognized the voice. He knew that the war between him and White would be brutal—and that it would not end until one of them lay dead.

White planned to let Pusser simmer in hostility while he went on a crime spree in Alabama. The death of Louise Hathcock had snapped White's shoelaces at the state line; he no longer had any connections at the Shamrock or the White Iris Club. The properties had been purchased by W. O. Hathcock, Jr., and Howard Bunch from Jack Hathcock's estate for $100,000. W. O. and Larice Hathcock attempted to operate the White Iris, but Buford Pusser rode herd on them until they closed shop.

The shakedown rackets at the border dwindled, but members of the state-line mob continued to feud with each other. On a narrow gravel road next to the Shamrock Motel, W. O. Hathcock, Jr., Hayward King, Lester Derrick, and Berry "Junior" Smith attempted to settle their differences with bullets. Hathcock and Smith suffered minor gunshot wounds. King was hospitalized with more than twenty-five pellets embedded in his head and body. Derrick escaped injury.

The gunfight had erupted when King, Smith, and Derrick attempted to use a road that Hathcock claimed was private property. The road provided the only access to a tract of land owned by King and Smith's wife, Shirley. It was located behind the Shamrock Motel in McNairy County.

Hathcock, who told Sheriff Buford Pusser that he had fired only after the three men started shooting at him, claimed the road was private. He contended that because he and Howard Bunch had purchased the Shamrock properties, the road, which had been built by Jack Hathcock, also belonged to him and his partner.

Pusser charged the hoodlums with disorderly conduct. Hayward King also filed an attempted-murder warrant against W. O. Hathcock, Jr.

Later, the disorderly conduct allegations were tossed out of court when the thugs refused to testify against each other. Hayward King also dropped the attempted murder charges against Hathcock.

Towhead White laughed to himself as he drove his Cadillac out of Corinth on U.S. 72 toward Alabama. "I'll bet that phone call I made to Pusser has him squirmin' in his shit. He's goin' crazy wonderin' what my next move will be," White chuckled aloud.

It was barely sundown when White arrived at the home of Dewitt Dawson in Leighton, Alabama. Dawson, the kingpin of organized crime in Alabama, had been in trouble with the law constantly since he was fifteen years old. He was sent to reform school for stealing gasoline in 1953 and had been in and out of federal and state prisons ever since. Law en-

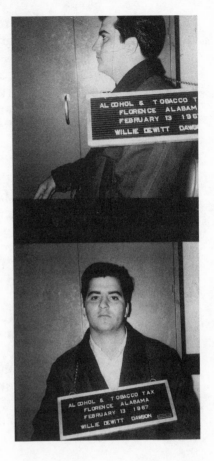

Dewitt Dawson, a close associate of Towhead White, is a north Alabama native. He is currently serving time in a federal prison on a variety of charges. Dawson was called the "worst outlaw in the state" by Alabama authorities.

forcement officials said that Dewitt Dawson had been involved in murder, drugs, robberies, and bootlegging.

Dawson and White had been friends for years. Like White, the six-foot, slender, black-haired Dawson had an irresistible personality. And also like White, the twenty-seven-year-old gangster was handsome and extremely popular with members of the opposite sex.

For the next few weeks, White and Dawson dabbled in a variety of criminal activities. Their specialty was robbing high-stake poker games.

Dawson, a polished gambler, often played cards with prominent businessmen and prosperous farmers in the north Alabama area. Most of the games required each player to have at least one thousand dollars in cash before the pasteboards were dealt around the table. It was not unusual for the gamblers to have from fifteen to forty thousand dollars among them.

White and Dawson practiced two styles of hijacking. On some occasions Dawson participated in the poker games. At a prearranged time, he visited the rest room, and on the way back to the card table, he would discreetly unlock the back door.

Minutes later, Towhead White, armed with a sawed-off shotgun, would storm into the room. During those escapades White usually wore a bright yellow sweat suit and a bird mask. He resembled a giant canary.

All the gamblers, including Dawson, would be forced to disrobe down to their underwear and toss their clothing into a pile in the middle of the floor. White would rake the money from the tabletop into a large burlap sack, scoop up the garments and stuff them into the bag, then flee. He always dropped Dawson's attire beside his partner's Lincoln Continental and waited for him at a designated spot down the road.

Other times, when Dawson was not one of the players, both he and White, wearing ski masks, rapped on the door and announced that they were the law. When the gamblers opened up, the shotgun-wielding bandits stripped their victims of their clothing and their money and disappeared into the night.

Finally, the authorities began breathing down the necks of White and Dawson, and Towhead moved back to Alcorn County. He owned a three-acre plot of land just off U.S. Highway 72 east of Corinth. He purchased a large mobile home and moved it onto his property. He also established a jukebox business in the trailer and called it White's Amusement Company.

Towhead learned through his old pal Nimbo Price that Buford Pusser had been asking about him. Pusser had frequently been seen in Corinth while White was in Alabama. "Let the sonofabitch sweat. He knows I'm gonna wipe his ass out sooner or later," White boasted to Price.

Both White and Pusser had ice water in their veins. Neither man was afraid of Satan himself, but they respected and feared each other.

Towhead White still had close ties to the Dixie Mafia. Even while he was working with Dewitt Dawson, he left for brief periods of time to perform criminal deeds with his Mafia colleagues.

While the band of outlaws had been successful in pulling off crimes and avoiding prosecution, the triumphs bred distrust among members of the brotherhood and triggered several cold-blooded murders within the Dixie Mafia ranks. A short time after White's return to Alcorn County, he agreed to "knock off" two fellow Dixie Mafia members.

On the night of November 27, 1968, Towhead White, Jerry Don Stewart, and George Albert McGann traveled to George Fuqua's apartment in Dallas, Texas. McGann had been a member of the Buford Pusser hit squad. Fuqua was a known strong-arm enforcer and a professional gambler.

Fuqua and Doris Ann Grooms, the wife of another Dixie Mafia thug, were kidnapped at gun point by White and his gang and driven to Plano, a small town about ten miles north of Dallas. Both victims were shot in the head and in the stomach. Their bodies were dumped alongside the highway.

According to inside sources, Fuqua and Mrs. Grooms had been skimming large sums of money from the "company pot." Towhead White and the two other killers were never linked to the homicides.

CHAPTER THIRTY

The mobile home squatted in a manicured yard with a backdrop of tall pines and poplars. It was cradled in an isolated area east of Corinth just off U.S. Highway 72. Towhead White's sleek Cadillac glistened in the light that shone from a night lamp perched atop a creosote pole beside the graveled driveway.

Sheriff Buford Pusser braked his unmarked Pontiac on the wrong side of the highway with all four wheels barely in White's drive. Snatching a machine gun from the seat beside him, he opened the door and climbed out.

The weapon jerked in Pusser's hands as he riddled the gangster's trailer from end to end. Belching flames lit up the yard. Exploding shells and smoldering slugs splitting metal made it sound as if Eliot Ness were raiding Al Capone's hideout. Then Pusser jumped into his car and sped away.

Towhead White, who was lying in bed at the time of the shooting, pressed his body flat against the mattress. He credited that maneuver with saving his life.

White heard Pusser's tires spew gravel, then squeal when they seized the pavement. The roar of the engine quickly faded in the distance.

The hoodlum scrambled from bed, dressed, and raced out to his car. He unlocked the trunk, removed a .30-.30 rifle, and headed toward Corinth. White knew that Pusser was long gone. Still, for more than two hours, he prowled the highway and the back roads near his residence.

The shooting caper was the subject of conversations for several days in Alcorn County. Pusser's name was not mentioned. Folks linked the violent escapade to disgruntled gangsters who were after Towhead White's scalp.

"It's a miracle ole Tow survived all them bullets slamming into his trailer. But he could ride through hell without gettin' a single hair on his head singed. He's the luckiest bastard that ever shit between a pair of shoes," said an old man who regularly lingered around the Alcorn County Courthouse.

This was not the first time Buford Pusser had left his calling card at Towhead White's pad. Less than a week before Pusser machine-gunned the outlaw's trailer, he had placed a huge death wreath on White's front door.

When White saw the funeral wreath, he left home and checked into a motel. For three nights in a row, he hid in a ditch across from his mobile home. Armed with a high-powered rifle, he waited for the McNairy County sheriff to return. Pusser never showed.

Towhead White had been wrangling with law enforcement officers ever since he was fourteen years old, but he had never locked horns with anyone like Buford Pusser. The other officers had stayed within the realm of the law when making arrests. To do otherwise could sometimes result in having cases thrown out of court. White knew that Pusser could not care less whether his tactics were legal. All Pusser cared about was getting the job done.

Buford Hayse Pusser was born on a sharecropper's cotton farm in McNairy County. The youngest of three offspring, he was delivered by a midwife on December 12, 1937, in a weather-beaten house near Finger, Tennessee.

While he was in the first grade, he allowed the other boys to push him around even though he was big for his age. Timid and shy, he quickly learned that to survive in a cruel world he would have to take a solid stand and fight for his rights. The instinct for survival soon became as much a part of Buford Pusser's life as the air he breathed.

When Buford was eleven years old, his parents, Carl and Helen Pusser, moved the family to Adamsville. After completing grammar school there, he entered Adamsville High, where he excelled in basketball and football. He graduated in 1956.

Afterward, he joined the Marine Corps, but frequent bouts with asthma cut his military career short. Back home with a medical discharge, Pusser landed a job with the Shackelford mortuary in Selmer. He drove ambulances and served as a part-time pallbearer. He comforted grief-stricken families before and after burials.

Pusser enjoyed his funeral home chores but found his small paychecks painful. When he was promised employment with top wages in Chicago, he left McNairy County and took a die cutter's job with the Union Bag Company.

There was something about death that intrigued Buford Pusser. In an effort to better understand his fascination with mortality, he enrolled in Worsham's College, a morticians' school in Chicago. He worked the day shift at the paper plant and attended classes at night. Eventually, the strain of keeping up with his studies at college while working a full shift at the factory became too much. The courses were also keeping his finances drained, so he withdrew from school.

Then Pusser found a way to earn extra money while keeping himself in top physical condition. He began wrestling professionally on weekends. At six feet, six inches, and 250 pounds, Buford Pusser was a natural crowd pleaser.

During one of the matches, he met a petite blonde Virginia native named Pauline Mullens. Divorced, with a small son and a daughter, she was three years older than Pusser. A whirlwind courtship followed.

On December 5, 1959, Buford and Pauline exchanged wedding vows. Before two years had passed, the Pussers became the parents of a baby girl.

Early in 1962, weakened by homesickness, Buford quit his job in Chicago and moved with Pauline and the children to Adamsville. He continued to wrestle, but the skirmishes on canvas provided barely enough money to keep his young family afloat. Regular jobs in the McNairy County area were as scarce as hens' teeth.

Finally, in October 1962, Pusser got a full-time job when his father resigned as Adamsville's police chief and recommended Buford for the post. It did not take Buford Pusser long to decide that law enforcement was his "cup of tea."

Now, Pusser had been sheriff of McNairy County for almost six years. During that time, he was forced to kill two persons in the line of duty. First, he had shot Louise

Hathcock. Then, on Christmas Day 1968, he killed an ex-convict named Charles Russell Hamilton. The sheriff shot Hamilton between the eyes with a .357 magnum after the former jailbird fired three .38-caliber bullets at Pusser when he answered a disturbance call at a Selmer duplex.

The price Pusser had paid for being sheriff was one that no man should ever have to pay. He knew that he would see Pauline die day after day for the rest of his life. And, when he shaved every morning, he felt the numbness of his own face, a face that plastic surgeons had spent months rebuilding after high-powered rifle slugs ripped it apart.

But Buford Pusser was even more pained by the vicious accusations that he had murdered his wife and shot himself to cover up the crime. The rumors, which circulated shortly after Pauline was slain, were made doubly painful because of his adulterous relationship with Pearl.

Investigators who sifted through the evidence said it would have been impossible for Buford Pusser to shoot Pauline and then blow half of his own face away with .30-.30 rifle slugs.

Pusser was convinced beyond any doubt that Towhead White had engineered the New Hope ambush. The sheriff was a firm believer in the biblical proverb, "an eye for an eye and a tooth for a tooth." Carl Douglas "Towhead" White owed Buford Pusser a full pound of flesh, and Pusser intended to collect every ounce.

After Pusser riddled White's trailer with bullet holes, the gangster moved from Alcorn County to the Southern Inn motel in Clarksdale, Mississippi. He became a partner with Police Chief Ben Collins in a jukebox racket. The Clarksdale Board of Commissioners later fired Collins after charging him with consorting with a known criminal. The commissioners also accused Collins of using his police chief post to pressure businessmen into taking jukeboxes owned by him and White.

An extraordinarily patient man, Buford Pusser was slowly baiting the Towhead White death trap. He had decided to offer the hoodlum a truce pact, and he wanted to make the peace offering in person. The sheriff did not trust secondhand information.

Actually, Pusser had no intention of trying to seal an authentic armistice with White. He wanted the gangster to believe the hatchet had been buried. Then "ole Tow" would be a vulnerable target when the curtain was ready to fall on the final act of the Towhead White drama.

Late one night, Pusser visited Corinth Police Chief Art Murphy and asked him to arrange a private meeting for the sheriff and the outlaw.

"I don't know if Tow will meet with you, Buford. He don't trust you worth a damn," Murphy told Pusser.

"Yeah. But he does trust you, Art. If you tell him I'm not gonna pull any shit on him, he'll believe you.

"I swear, Art, I just wanna try and talk some sense into him," Pusser assured Murphy. "If we keep on actin' like the Hatfields and the McCoys, one of us is gonna end up in the graveyard."

"I damn well know it, Buford. You two guys need to settle your differences in a peaceful manner. I like both of you. I know it irritates you, but I like ole Tow, too."

"That's your business, Art. After I have a heart-to-heart talk with him, I might learn to like him, too," Pusser lied.

Murphy, who was sitting in a chair behind his desk, pushed himself back and stood. "I might be able to persuade Tow to meet with you. But you gotta give me your word now, Buford, you won't get him alone and shoot him."

Pusser laughed. "Hell, no! I just wanna make peace with him before one of us gets killed."

"Let me see what I can do. You boys do need to clear the air between you. I'll talk to Tow, then give you a call," Murphy promised.

On the way back to Selmer, Pusser detected a skip in his Pontiac's firing system. It annoyed him. He relished fast cars and flawless engines.

The sheriff sometimes tested his Pontiac's performance against Larry Price's 1966 Chevrolet Caprice. The "Black Phantom" Chevy had a 427 turbojet engine. For a long while Pusser had been racing his cars against the Price-driven Caprice. Buford had never outrun Price's automobile, but the speed contests allowed him to keep his cars checked out.

Now, traveling along U.S. 45 with the engine output worsening, Pusser decided to park his Pontiac in front of the Sibley Chevrolet garage in Selmer and summon a deputy to take him home. He especially wanted the Pontiac to be in top running condition during the next few days.

On March 6, 1969, at 2:30 P.M., Towhead White met Buford Pusser at the Holiday Inn parking lot in Corinth. White got into Pusser's car. They left the motel and headed east.

Agents of the Mississippi Alcoholic Beverage Control (A.B.C.) were shocked when they spotted Pusser and the ex-convict together. Officers B. F. Blakeney, A. B. Marlar, and Julian Bomar were in Corinth to investigate liquor violations.

Agent Bomar reported the incident in a letter to A.B.C. headquarters in Jackson. "At approximately 2:30 P.M. on March 6, 1969, Carl Douglas "Towhead" White was seen in the car with Sheriff Buford Pusser of McNairy County, Tennessee. Pusser was driving a black 1968 Pontiac with Tennessee license plate number 1420." The letter, dated March 7, 1969, was signed "Julian Bomar, Enforcement Agent."

Buford Pusser never knew that the Mississippi liquor agents had seen him with Towhead White.

Pusser was setting the hoodlum up like a clay pigeon on a skeet thrower. The sheriff's plans to rid society of Towhead White were right on schedule.

Meanwhile, the A.B.C. agents hit pay dirt. On March 8, they raided the El-Ray Motel in Corinth and arrested Junior Smith. Smith was charged with possession of whiskey and beer for reselling without a license. He was released on bond. Less than three weeks later, Shirley Smith was arrested in a house trailer near the motel on similar charges.

The Smiths also owned the Old Hickory Club near Guys, Tennessee, in McNairy County. They bootlegged whiskey there as well.

The large roadhouse was stuck in a clump of pine trees off a rural road about a mile from U.S. Highway 45. Motorcycle gang members were regular visitors at the place.

Marijuana had crept into the area, and grass smoking was a popular pastime at the Old Hickory. While Junior Smith did not allow anyone to puff marijuana inside the building, it was permitted around the picnic tables in the back yard.

Sheriff Buford Pusser made frequent visits to the Old Hickory Club, and he could have nabbed law violators there every day. But he did not ride herd on Junior Smith or his customers.

Berry "Junior" Smith owed Buford Pusser a string of personal favors. Pusser would soon ask Smith to clear his account.

CHAPTER THIRTY-ONE

The yellow line running down the middle of Highway 72 kept weaving on and off the road. At least, that's what Towhead White thought. He was drunk.

White was driving back to Corinth from north Alabama. Beside him on the front seat of the new green Chrysler was Shirley Smith. It was April 2, 1969.

Towhead and Shirley had been drinking whiskey at the home of Dewitt Dawson in Leighton, Alabama. During the visit, White tried to shoot out a naked light bulb dangling from the ceiling of an old house located behind Dawson's colonial-style mansion. The old building was used to warehouse whiskey and beer for Dawson's far-flung bootlegging business. White, an expert marksman, emptied his five-shot .38-caliber Smith & Wesson at the bulb. Liquor caused him to miss the target all five times.

Now, traveling recklessly toward Mississippi, Towhead and Shirley had just left Arnold's Truck Stop, located on U.S. 72 near Muscle Shoals, Alabama, where they had eaten southern-fried catfish dinners. Before leaving the restaurant, Shirley Smith made a telephone call from a pay booth.

Earlier that morning, after eating breakfast at Ben Collins' house, White had driven from Clarksdale to Corinth. Upon his arrival he learned that Howard Carroll's body had been found floating in Elam Creek near the Sandy's Lumber shed in Corinth. Authorities said the sixty-four-year-old Carroll was intoxicated when he wandered into the narrow stream of water and drowned. Police counted sixteen empty wine bottles on the creek bank.

Towhead White had been extremely fond of the old state-line wino. He immediately went to McPeters Funeral Home and made arrangements to pay Howard Carroll's nine hundred dollar burial expenses. White told McPeters that he would return later that day and settle the debt. He had a wad of cash in his pocket but for some reason chose to delay the squaring of Carroll's funeral bill.

After leaving the mortuary, White hooked up with Shirley Smith. She had telephoned him the night before and had asked him to come to Corinth. Towhead and Shirley were long-time friends.

The Chrysler streaked across the Alabama–Mississippi state line on U.S. 72 toward Iuka, Burnsville, and Corinth. Shirley Smith shifted nervously on the passenger seat. Towhead White was still having trouble tracking the yellow line in the center of the highway.

A lone assassin was waiting patiently on the roof of the El-Ray Motel. Time dragged. He would be relieved when his job was finally completed.

Alcorn County Deputy Sheriff Hobert Bingham points to the fatal bullet hole in the windshield of Towhead White's Chrysler after the hoodlum was murdered on April 3, 1969, in Corinth.

Just after midnight White parked the Chrysler in front of Room 3 at the El-Ray. Shirley Smith scooted against the right door. The "hit" man skillfully aimed a .30-.30 rifle at the hoodlum's head and squeezed the trigger. The slug smashed through the windshield and slammed into White's forehead, jerking his body back on the seat. Blood gushed from an ugly bullet hole just above Towhead's eyebrows. In the motel parking area, several more gunshots echoed in the still night air.

Almost before the gunsmoke had settled, Alcorn County Sheriff Grady Bingham received a call at his home in Corinth. Barbara Bivens, who lived in a house trailer next door to the motel, told Bingham, "There's a lotta shootin' goin' on at the El-Ray." Then she quickly hung up.

Tommy Bivens, who was visiting with his ex-wife at the time, walked with her over toward the El-Ray to investigate. They remained on the shoulder of U.S. 45 in front of the motel. Junior Smith was standing by the driver's side of the Chrysler.

"What happened, Junior?" Bivens hollered from the road.

"I just killed ole Tow. Come on over and look," Smith urged.

Bivens refused to budge. He did not trust Junior Smith or Towhead White, and he wondered if it might be a trap. Bivens was afraid that White might be "playing 'possum," that the gangster would rise up and blast him into eternity if he approached the car. Bivens had not been close to White since that night at the Shamrock when the outlaw had tried to kill him.

Within minutes, the sheriff and his brother, Chief Deputy Hobert Bingham, arrived at the scene. The sheriff slid from the car and strolled toward Smith, who was standing beside the bullet-riddled Chrysler. "What's goin' on here, Junior?"

"I think I've killed Towhead White. He was drunk and shot at me. He shot first."

Sheriff Bingham opened the door on the driver's side. White was slumped back in the seat. Blood covered most of his face and chest. Pink bubbles occasionally leaked from a large hole near the center of his forehead. His brown eyes were wide open.

An interior view of the 1969 Chrysler in which Towhead White was murdered. White was sitting behind the steering wheel when the fatal shot was fired through the windshield.

The sheriff removed a .38-caliber pistol from White's left hand. There were two spent cartridges in the cylinder.

"Call an ambulance," Bingham ordered. But he knew there was no reason to hurry. Carl Douglas "Towhead" White was dead.

County Coroner George Coleman arrived with an ambulance and transported White's body to the Magnolia Hospital. Dr. H. D. Gray inspected and X-rayed the corpse; then Coleman took the remains to his funeral home. Gray said White had been shot in the head, the collarbone, and the right arm with high-powered rifle bullets. According to the doctor, the shot to the head caused instant death.

"Where's the murder weapon, Junior?" Bingham asked.

"It's in the office. I'll get it." Smith, with the sheriff on his heels, went into the registration area of the motel. He lifted a .30-.30 rifle from a nearby bed and handed it to Bingham.

"You say you shot Towhead, Junior?"

"I had to do it, Sheriff. He fired at me first."

"Well, you're under arrest for murder. Go on and get in my car. I'll take you to jail in a few minutes." Bingham knew that Smith would be as meek as a lamb around him. The outlaw did not want to stir the coals of an already smoldering fire.

Chief Deputy Hobert Bingham was instructed to guard the Chrysler and keep all spectators away from it until the sheriff returned from the jail.

Junior Smith told Grady Bingham that the shooting had erupted when Towhead and Shirley arrived at the motel and White began calling Smith a "motherfucker" and firing at him with the pistol.

Smith said he ducked, then turned and ran into the office of the motel, where he grabbed the .30-.30 rifle. Another bullet, Smith claimed, whizzed past his head as he leveled the rifle at White's car. Shirley, according to Smith, saw the raised rifle in her husband's hands and struggled to get the passenger door open. When she failed, she took cover on the floorboard just as a bullet shattered the windshield. Shirley finally pushed open the door and leaped from the car.

Smith said he crouched low as he ran down the sidewalk and fired the rifle at White's Chrysler again. He claimed he then jerked a .357 magnum from his belt and drilled three holes through the right door of the vehicle.

After listening to Smith's version of the slaying, Bingham locked him in a jail cell and returned to the El-Ray Motel. Blood and brains were splattered all over the Chrysler's interior. The car had been riddled by nine bullets; six were rifle slug holes. Bingham knew that the first bullet through the windshield had been the fatal shot.

A blood-splotched canvas bag, full of quarters White had taken from his jukeboxes, lay behind the seat on the driver's side. Bingham thought the silver coins were probably the only honest money the gangster had ever possessed.

The two-door 1969 green Chrysler, bearing Coahoma County, Mississippi, license plate number 14D1598, was registered to White's sister, Rachell Beard of Clarksdale.

Bingham questioned Shirley Smith at the motel. Her story was a carbon copy of her husband's account of the killing.

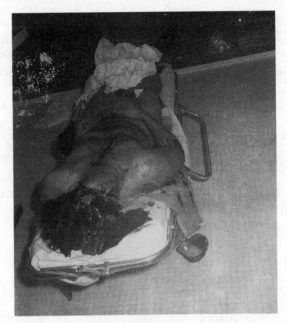

The bullet-riddled corpse of Towhead
White lies on a gurney at the Coleman Funeral Home in Corinth.

"Well, I appreciate the interview. I've gotta take White's car to the jail. You got something I can sit on? That seat is covered with blood," Bingham frowned.

Shirley Smith went into the motel office and returned with a thick fabric cushion. Bingham thanked her, placed the pillow under the steering wheel of the Chrysler, and climbed in. During the short jaunt to the Alcorn County Jail, blood soaked through the cushion onto Bingham's trousers. He had to go home, take a bath, and change clothes before he went to the funeral home to examine White's body.

Grady Bingham stared for several minutes at the naked corpse of Towhead White. He had a strange feeling about the homicide. The sheriff was convinced that Junior Smith was not the triggerman. He was also sure that Smith was one canary that would never sing.

George Coleman had removed an expensive gold watch from White's left arm and a large diamond ring from his right hand. A search of White's clothing turned up $5.72.

His billfold was empty. The five bills and 72¢ in coins were found in the right front pocket of his dove-gray dress pants. White's long-sleeved navy-blue sport shirt yielded a mere pack of cigarettes.

Grady Bingham was surprised to find only $5.72 in White's pockets. The hoodlum usually carried enough greenbacks on him to open a small bank.

Bingham and Coleman next called on White's mother at her house in Corinth. She and her youngest daughter, Pat, had moved from the Clarksdale area to Corinth shortly before Towhead's parole from prison. Bingham rapped on the front door.

Elizabeth White, pale and shaken over the violent death of her only son, answered the knock. Bingham and Coleman introduced themselves.

"I'm Carl's mother. I guess you're glad he's dead, Sheriff!" Mrs. White snapped.

"No, ma'am. I'm never happy when anybody dies. But your son ran with the wrong crowd, and that bunch wasn't my kind of people." Bingham did not want to tell the woman how he really felt about her son's demise. He realized that she could not help the fact that Carl Douglas "Towhead" White had turned out to be one of the most ruthless gangsters in the United States. His death sparked a giant celebration in the law enforcement camp.

"Carl was a good boy!" Mrs. White insisted. "The police never gave him a chance. They rode his back day and night."

George Coleman interrupted. He was a short, rotund man who wore glasses and smoked a pipe. Coleman had a gentle personality. "We're sorry about your son's death, Mrs. White. Here's his watch and ring. Thought you'd want them."

"Yes. Thank you. Thank you very much," she replied, taking the jewelry and clutching it in her left hand.

"His body is at my funeral home. Do you want me to handle the arrangements for you?" asked Coleman.

"No. I appreciate your concern, Mr. Coleman. But Bill McPeters was a close friend of Carl's. I want him to handle the funeral."

"That's okay. I'll call Bill when I get back to my office," Coleman assured her.

Ironically, the corpses of Towhead White and Howard Carroll were in McPeters Funeral Home at the same time. White had promised Bill McPeters early on April 2 that he would return later that day to the funeral home and pay Carroll's burial expenses. White had returned, but he would never again conduct any kind of business.

On Thursday night, April 3, many persons paid their final respects to Towhead White. Friends and curiosity seekers filed past White's closed bronze casket in an upstairs parlor at the McPeters Mortuary.

Early the next morning, while McPeters was preparing to take White's body to Clarksdale for funeral services and burial, Bobby Anderson, Louise Hathcock's nephew, paid Grady Bingham a visit at the sheriff's office. "Hello, Sheriff. I wanted to pick up Tow's money. Me and him was workin' together in the jukebox business," said Anderson.

Bingham dragged open a large bottom drawer and removed a sack of quarters, a billfold, and an envelope containing $5.72. "There it is," Bingham frowned as he placed the items on top of the desk.

Anderson quickly flipped open the wallet, then peered into the envelope. "Where's the rest of his money?"

"That's it. I don't know how much is in the bag. I didn't count it."

"Somebody has robbed Tow," fumed Anderson. "He had a lotta money on him when he came to Corinth Wednesday mornin'. Somebody cleaned him out!"

"That may be true. But that's all the money he had on him when we took his body outta the car," replied Bingham.

Rumors quickly spread that Buford Pusser had instigated White's murder. Some even said he was the triggerman. Newsmen questioned the sheriff about the allegations.

"I didn't shoot Towhead White. I would have shot him if he had ever given me the opportunity," said Pusser. "White was like a poisonous snake. He needed killing."

Almost everyone agreed that if Pusser had masterminded White's death, it was a valid case of justifiable homicide.

Services for Towhead White were held on the afternoon

of Friday, April 4, at the National Funeral Home in Clarksdale. A soloist sang "In the Garden" and "My God and I." The Reverend Leroy Tubbs gave a brief message. The preacher could not, in good faith, spend much time talking about Towhead White shaking hands with Saint Peter at the pearly gates.

A horde of gangsters, wearing five hundred dollar suits and smoking expensive cigars, attended White's funeral. Ben Collins was one of the pallbearers. Carl Douglas "Towhead" White was laid to rest in Clarksdale's Memorial Gardens.

Berry "Junior" Smith was still in the Alcorn County Jail in lieu of a fifteen thousand dollar bond. Finally, on April 9, he was bailed out by his wife and her relatives. Peace Justice Moody Brawner ordered Smith to appear two days later for a preliminary hearing. Brawner asked Justices Herman Baker and Erskin Rowsey to assist him with the case.

Smith, wearing a crisp green suit and a yellow sweater, pleaded innocent to murdering Towhead White. His attorneys, David Coleman and Floyd Cunningham, insisted that their client had shot the flamboyant outlaw in self-defense. The Alcorn County grand jury later agreed and refused to indict Smith.

"I brought the sonofabitch to Corinth, and I sent the sonofabitch home," Smith boasted after the no-bill. Smith and White had come to Alcorn County together from the Mississippi Delta in 1953.

Many persons close to the case, including Sheriff Grady Bingham, did not believe that Junior Smith was the one who killed Towhead White. The skeptics maintained that Smith had staged the "shoot-out" at the motel to cover the tracks of the real assassin. According to police detectives, Junior Smith's story about White's slaying had more holes in it than the late gangster's bullet-riddled Chrysler did.

The fatal shot through the windshield was fired down from a high angle, not from ground level as Smith had claimed. The pistol White supposedly used was found in his left hand although he was right-handed. The outlaw, who was an expert shot with his right hand, would have slid from the car and crouched behind the front fender for protection. The engine would have provided a solid fortress. White was not drunk enough, or stupid enough, to make himself an open target by leaning out a car window with a revolver in his left hand. Grady Bingham said that the weapon was definitely placed in White's hand after he had died.

Furthermore, the pistol was registered to Shirley Smith. Investigators failed to locate any other guns on White or in his car. It would have been easier to catch the pope stark naked in Vatican Square than to catch Towhead White without his own side arm. Authorities believed that Shirley Smith had coaxed the intoxicated criminal into giving her his pistol after he attempted to shoot out the light bulb in Dewitt Dawson's joint.

Sheriff Bingham admitted that neither he nor the other investigators had actually tried to unearth the true facts surrounding White's murder. "To be absolutely honest, we didn't really give a damn who killed Towhead White," said Bingham. "With the bastard gone, we had a big-time criminal out of circulation."

Information gleaned from investigators and other inside sources unraveled an intriguing story about the assassination of Carl Douglas "Towhead" White. McNairy County Sheriff Buford Pusser was the chief architect of the murder plot. He had vowed for two years to even the score with White for the New Hope Road ambush that left the sheriff's wife a corpse and him on the threshold of death.

Berry "Junior" Smith owed Pusser several favors. The sheriff had deliberately looked the other way while law violations thrived at Smith's Old Hickory Club. Pusser had wanted Smith indebted to him.

Smith was a tailor-made fall guy. Both he and White were criminals. Law enforcement officers never came unglued when one gangster bumped off another one. And White trusted Smith. Junior could have easily lured Towhead into a trap.

On Wednesday, April 2, 1969, the trap was baited. Shirley Smith planned to party with White until just after dark, then have him drive her to the El-Ray Motel. The plan jumped the track when White suddenly decided to visit Dewitt Dawson in Alabama.

Before leaving Arnold's Truck Stop in Muscle Shoals, Shirley Smith telephoned her husband at the motel. She ex-

THE STATE-LINE MOB • 189

Grady Bingham, former sheriff of Alcorn County, helped to investigate the murder of Towhead White. He has always maintained that Junior Smith, who confessed to slaying White, was not the triggerman.

plained the delay and told him that she and Towhead were on their way back to Corinth. They were expecting the trip to take less than two hours.

White had ninety thousand dollars in cash locked in the trunk of the Chrysler. Most of the money had come from a robbery and a "hit" job in Texas. He also had a large roll of greenbacks in his front pants pocket.

The sniper, who had been recruited by Junior Smith, waited for his victim for almost an hour on the motel roof. When Towhead and Shirley parked in front of Room 3, the rifleman drilled a hole in White's forehead with a .30-.30 slug. Then he tossed the weapon down to Smith, who fired five more bullets into White's automobile. Smith also shot three holes in the right door of the vehicle with a .357 magnum.

White's final curtain call had been in the planning stages for weeks. Pusser had sealed a pact with Junior Smith to rid society of the notorious gangster. Under Towhead White's well-groomed hair was a scalp that the McNairy County sheriff wanted with a compulsive passion.

* * *

Buford Pusser propped his elbows on his desk and steepled the fingers of his huge freckled hands. He gazed at the diamond ring on the smallest finger on his left hand. The cluster of stones that adorned it had been taken from three rings Pauline had worn. Shortly after she was murdered, Pusser had a jeweler fashion the ring for him. It was a constant reminder that he still had much unfinished business with his wife's killers.

It was almost 12:15 A.M. when the telephone shattered the silence in the sheriff's private office, located in the courthouse basement in Selmer. Pusser answered.

"Buford?"

"Yeah."

"Towhead White is history."

EPILOGUE

Today the Tennessee–Mississippi border is as peaceful as a rural cemetery. But the haunting memories of the old state-line mob are still very much alive.

Kirksey McCord Nix, Jr., one of the hoodlums Buford Pusser named as his wife's assassins, is presently serving a life sentence in a Louisiana state prison. He was convicted of armed robbery and murdering a New Orleans grocer. Only recently, Nix was indicted on several counts of conspiracy and theft in a mail-extortion scam conducted from behind bars. He has also been linked to the murders of Mississippi Judge Vincent Sherry and his wife, Margaret. Authorities claim Nix arranged for one of the Dixie Mafia thugs to do the "hit" jobs.

Dewitt Dawson, Towhead White's old pal, is still up to his same tricks. He is serving time in a federal slammer for a variety of charges ranging from possession of illegal firearms to counterfeiting.

Some of the surviving members of the state-line mob—including Junior and Shirley Smith, Tommy Bivens, and W. O. Hathcock, Jr., and his wife, Larice—still live in Corinth, Mississippi.

Hayward King, who now attends church regularly, lives in McNairy County, Tennessee.

Billy Garrett was killed in a plane crash on February 19, 1976.

The three other gunmen Pusser said were involved with Kirksey Nix, Jr., in the New Hope Road ambush are dead. Carmine Raymond Gagliardi's body, riddled with gangster bullets, was found floating in Boston Harbor. Gary Elbert

191

McDaniel and George Albert McGann were both found shot to death in Texas.

Corinth Police Chief Art Murphy was killed on March 1, 1973, by Police Captain Jerry McDaniel. According to official records, Murphy was drunk when he fired at McDaniel and Police Lieutenant Tommy Inman. The homicide was ruled self-defense.

Former Clarksdale Police Chief Ben Collins, who resides in Lambert, Mississippi, is in failing health.

Ex-Alcorn County Justice of the Peace Buck Sorrell married Fannie Bell Barker, Phenix City's former "Queen of Hearts." They live in the Nashville, Tennessee, area.

Sheriff Grady Bingham is happily retired from law enforcement and living in Corinth with his wife.

Buford Pusser died in a fiery car crash on August 21, 1974, near his hometown of Adamsville, Tennessee. His life story was the subject of at least two books, and his exploits were also portrayed in three *Walking Tall* movies.

Employing the same criminal tactics that the state-line mob used, Buford Pusser played an important role in helping to purify the Tennessee–Mississippi border. But Pusser did not wipe out the corruption single-handedly. The gangsters themselves slowly eradicated the crime at the state line. They kept murdering one another until there were no ringleaders left.